WHEN YOU'RE READY

THIS
is
HOW
you
HEAL

A COLLECTION OF ESSAYS

BRIANNA WIEST

THOUGHT
CATALOG
Books

THOUGHTCATALOG.COM
NEW YORK · LOS ANGELES

THOUGHT CATALOG Books

Copyright © 2022 Brianna Wiest.
All rights reserved.

Published by Thought Catalog Books, an imprint of the digital magazine Thought Catalog, which is owned and operated by The Thought & Expression Company LLC, an independent media organization based in Brooklyn, New York and Los Angeles, California.

This book was produced by Chris Lavergne and Noelle Beams with art direction and design by KJ Parish. Special thanks to Isidoros Karamitopoulos for circulation management.

thoughtcatalog.com | shopcatalog.com

Made in the USA

ISBN 978-1-949759-44-0

For the ones who face a fork in the road...

There is only one path:
the one that leads you
to your truth.

TABLE
of
CONTENTS

INTRODUCTION

Healing is not a one-time event.

It can begin with a one-time event—typically some form of sudden loss that disrupts our projection of what the future might be. However, the true work of healing is allowing that disruption to wake us from a deep state of unconsciousness, to release the personas we adapted into and begin consciously piecing together the full truth of who we were meant to be.

The experiences that catalyze healing are not trying to prompt us to simply recover from a blow to the ego, but for the first time, in many cases, to recognize our ego at all. It is a moment of reconciliation where we are asked to realize that, in the words of Michael Murphy, "a greater life is pressing to be born."

If we do not answer this call, it will continue to show up in our lives, often in similar patterns and feelings. We will continuously return to wondering: "*How am I still here?*" or "*How did I get here again?*" The answer is that the same wake-up call keeps coming in until our subconscious minds agree to embark on the journey of our own becoming. This is a process of fully restoring us into remembrance of the perfect, whole and complete truth of who we are. It is a life-long quest, because we must tend to the gardens of our minds on a daily basis. Like children, they cannot completely manage themselves. Our lives require a higher functioning, future-considering adult aspect of ourselves to come forth and sit in the driver's seat.

This is a journey because no healing, whether physical or spiritual, is something that occurs linearly, nor seamlessly. Life contracts before it expands, and pulls back before it leaps forward. This balancing act is not something we should resist, but rather, embrace. The longer we avoid doing so, the longer we will dwell on the event or series of events that arose on our paths for the sake of waking us up, rather than truly beginning the more difficult, but far more rewarding, work.

In many ways, the journey of healing is not so much a chapter in your story, but changing the way you write the entire book. It's a shift in the way you move through the world, one in which you move from being disappointed that life has not met your every expectation to expanding your vision to perceive all of the magic, the wonder, the awe, the heartache, the loss, the gain, the contrast that makes us all perfectly and unpredictably human.

Our healed selves are not our most flawless selves. They are not immune to sadness or grief or fear. They are just not controlled by those experiences any longer. They feel sadness when it is time for sadness, and grief when it is time to grieve, and contentment on a more regular basis. They fear things that are unknown or important or both, but they do not allow that emotion to prevent them from moving forward. Life can be deeply challenging and profoundly unfair, and without the ability to move through the feelings that may accompany our experiences in real time, we often become trapped in the old stories we once wove around them.

When we are able to validate, accept and process our own human experience independent of anyone else, something magical occurs. We begin reconnecting with our true desires, heeding our subtlest instincts, and cease sabotaging our inspired thoughts and feelings. Through this, we tend to usher in a serendipitous unfolding of events. Over time, we begin to recognize that there is a common thread carrying us through each one of these experiences, which is our soul's silent guidance: ever-present, and always leading us just beyond what we can see in real time.

As we start to recognize this power, we begin to trust it more. As we start to trust it more, we begin to follow it more closely. We have greater stretches of feeling ease and and love. Our lives begin to come back into harmony through our new grounded, centered perspective. We realize that we were never really lost, we were just giving ourselves some space to process before we could move forward completely.

Your first purpose is to heal.

The sheer impact of you becoming the person you know you were meant to be will have a ripple effect on everyone and everything around you. Nothing will ever be the same. If you cannot imagine how else you might leave a legacy, help others, or do something meaningful with your life, the most important place to start is within yourself.

It's also the hardest place to start.

It's far simpler to gaze outward and point our fingers at what we believe everyone else is doing wrong. It is more challenging to look ourselves in the mirror and be honest about the ways that we have not been living up to our true potential, to identify the areas in life where we have some room for growth, and then to consistently push ourselves to show up every day to make those changes manifest.

When we claim ownership over the unique destiny that is meant to be ours, the collective heals with us, because we are all pieces of the whole. Perfection will be impossible, as it is within the contrast that this world becomes what it is meant to be—a training ground for soul development. This is not about trying to take the world and make it what we think its most perfect iteration might be, but to finally do what we had intended all along: to awaken, to remember, to witness our own seeds of potential take root.

In the same way that no two people are exactly alike, every purpose we are called to is unique as well, and this is precisely what this book intends to do: awaken each of us to the small and large ways in which we truly can affect those around us, in the corner of the earth we were given, in the specific ways we know how, for the period of time that is ours.

You are far from alone in hearing the call to wake up from the life you had planned in order to commit wholeheartedly to the life that has been waiting. If enough of us are able to do so, I believe we will have the potential to see massive shifts in our shared physical reality. There is not one person who does not need healing, because there is not one person who does not need to be awakened from their unconsciousness and into all life might offer.

This book is a collection of pieces I wrote over the course of many years of my own journey, beginning as a young girl who suffered from significant mental and emotional health disorders, to the woman sitting on the coast of California on a chilly summer evening—healthy, established, connected and thriving—and writing these words to you now.

If you picked up this book, you're already on that same path to healing and discovering your true purpose. I hope my words may help ease your heart through the journey your brave soul has already begun.

See you on the other side.

Brianna Wiest
January 2022

WHEN
YOU'RE
READY,
this is how
YOU HEAL

You recognize that familiar, dull feeling in your gut—as though something is wrong, though you can't quite pinpoint what. You start to take inventory of your life. You recount your job, your salary, your friends, what so-and-so from such-and-such time in your life would think of you now, your nice new profile photo on Facebook. The pieces, when put together, form a picture that should nullify that feeling.

And yet.

You go through life stymied by that ache. It crescendos and crashes. You get distracted by the news or your job or Twitter, or something that temporarily scares you a little bit more.

It goes on, until one day, you realize you're being levied, haunted, by a pain you can't quite decipher. Slowly, it wears you down. It's harder to get up. It's harder to go out. It's easier to drink and then drink some more. Or maybe eat, or shop, or post photos of yourself to Instagram. Everyone has a different vice.

The more you are confused by the small, scary feeling you can't figure out, the worse it gets. And the worse it gets, the more you become convinced that it's a warning of what is to come. You start to attach thoughts to the feeling, fear stories.

The stories, you realize, are illogical. You're overreacting. You're convinced your world is imminently coming to an end and these "gut feelings," the ones you've been implicitly told to trust for so long, are simply warning you to take cover.

What you can't see right now is that nothing is really wrong.

Actually, things are really right, which is why you finally feel safe enough to feel what you really feel. Stop projecting. Stop telling stories. Those dull, unsettling feelings are not in the future—they're in the past.

You've been carrying them with you all this time.

If we don't finish processing our emotional experiences, they stay with us like the food we can't metabolize, or old clothes we never get around to packing up and putting out at the curb. Sometimes, they hold within them nourishment, wisdom and guidance. Other times, they're debris from a chapter long closed.

Either way, they are signals to the spaces in which we are not yet free.

When you're ready to heal, you will need to lay yourself down in a very safe space and focus on those tense feelings. Have them show you their origins. You will begin to see moments you forgot about, feelings you forgot you ever felt. The past will come up in blinks and vignettes. Slowly, over time, you will awaken to what is really wrong—which is the piece of you that had to break off and build a wall around your heart because behind it was a wound you did not yet know how to heal.

When you are ready, you will step behind it.

You will know that the anger, the sadness, and the anxiety are a veil, a trigger trying to wake you up, not knock you out.

You will need to cry. You will need to cry for the 13-year-old that got her heart broken, for the 16-year-old whose friends were mean to him. You will need to mourn what you lost and when you lost it. You will need to go back in time and insert yourself into those memories as an adult and tell your child self to say what they really needed to say at the moment they needed to say it, though they couldn't find the words or the courage. You will need to do this, over and over again, until you slowly realize you are becoming lighter. You are releasing. Though you cannot change time, you are, somehow, changing your story.

You will need to sweat. You will need to stretch and move your body, and pay close attention to where you are tight and what feels uncomfortable, and where you are pent up and storing all that pain.

You will need to shake. You will need to lay on the floor and literally shake out everything you're holding. You will need to let yourself feel vulnerable and small—both of which are, at the end of the day, the two feelings we guard ourselves against the most.

You will need to surrender. Through the tears and sweat and shaking and shifting, you will stop fighting it. You will see your past life for what it was, so you can see your present life for what it is: filled with hope and potential.

Eventually, you will get up, and your world will start to change.

You will exit relationships and begin others. You will call someone you haven't talked to in a long time. You will suddenly be inspired to attend a new class, or find yourself drafting your resignation email. You will begin writing, reading, sitting outside, and drinking water, feeling grateful for these simple, nourishing things. You will sleep a bit easier. Gradually, you will start to return to yourself. You will enter that emotional fire and burn off everything blocking the core of you from truly being in the world.

Then you will know that when you lose someone, you must cry.

When you're frustrated, you must be frustrated.

When you want to say something, you must speak.

In the healing process, you don't just learn how to go back and fix what you didn't finish. You also learn how to press forward, how to live more intently and presently, how to process your experiences in real-time. The more you do this, the more you will awaken and begin to show up for life. You start speaking again, you start feeling again, you start *being* again.

When you feel strong enough to look at what's wrong, you begin to unearth your soul.

It was always there. It was just buried under years and layers of identities and styles and beliefs and ideas that had adhered themselves to you like a shield.

You were never lost.

You were only hidden.

All the time you spent feeling so uncomfortable was just your deepest self trying to speak to you, trying to remind you of its presence.

It was only the core of you saying: *Keep going. There is more to life than this.*

WHEN YOU *are* READY *to* CHANGE YOUR LIFE, READ THIS

What if, in the moments you feel most alone, you begin to realize that you are also free?

What if you could see that in these very moments you fear most, you are also completely unburdened from the expectations of others, able to define and redefine yourself, to explore life on your own terms, to hear the sound of your own voice? What if being on your own, in any capacity, is a sign of self-sufficiency and courage? What if you've already made it? What if instead of believing your aloneness is a sign you have failed, you realize that it is proof you have accomplished the most daring task of all?

What if, instead of believing that your job is not enough—in compensation, in status, in whatever you've chalked your inferiority up to be—you began to realize that no set of tasks could ever define the whole of who you are? What if you began to understand that a job is a means to an end, and you doing anything to contribute to your or your family's well-being and security is important and yet only one facet of success? What if instead of believing that you must be the best to be good enough, you realized that to have somewhere to wake up and go, something to wake up and do, is a purpose and gift that should never be taken for granted?

What if, instead of believing that you have failed, you began to recognize that failure is just life's way of moving you in another direction? What if instead of counting up all the times things haven't worked out precisely the way you imagined they would or should, you considered that perhaps you were being led somewhere better? What if you found awe and reverence in the fact that there is a force so powerful protecting you—perhaps one you cannot even name or see or even believe in—that is refusing to let you have even the things you beg hardest for because there is something else you are so destined for?

What if instead of thinking that your life was meant to unfold seamlessly, you realized that the courage it takes to keep opening doors, even if they all close, is all part of the process?

What if, instead of losing hope in the world and life itself, you allowed your failures to strengthen your faith, making you see that there is a path for you to walk, and a forcefield holding you to it, no matter how hard you may try to get off?

What if, instead of begrudging someone for not being precisely the person you imagined they would be, you realize that the offering of someone's time is the ultimate sacrifice and the epitome of love? What if you realized that they are under no obligation to be who you think they should be, and the most loving thing you could do would be to set them free of the expectations you hold in your own mind? What if you realized that they don't have to be just as you imagine in order for you to exchange the love you are meant to share? What if the gift you're receiving right now is the chance to witness the rawness of someone's heart, their edges and imperfections? What if the journey is really asking you to love a flawed person, so you might be able to love your own flaws the same way?

What if the life of your dreams is not one where you do all things perfectly for an audience within your own imagination, but one where you have a few things you care about deeply and passionately and spend your life tending to them, releasing into the nothingless all the other cares that did nothing but hold you back from your own love and life?

What if your body appears precisely the way it is meant to, but you are so busy focusing on the flaws that nobody else notices, you're overlooking the beauty everyone else sees? What if you believe that there's something wrong with the way you look because you've spent an excessive amount of time fantasizing about how light and free perfection would feel? What if all you needed to do was simply look around you? To the people you know, the people you don't, the people who coexist in the world beside you? What if you truly began to realize that almost nobody exists within that fantasy, and yet so many are still deeply and completely loved, fully alive and happy, walking in their truth and thriving as all they were meant to be?

I'm not saying that there aren't real problems in your life, only that it's very hard to actually identify those problems when you're so busy trying to correct non-issues, so preoccupied with questions that have no answers. You could spend your entire lifetime wondering if you are worthy and enough and beautiful and successful and you will never come up with anything concrete. So you have a choice. You have a choice of how you will build your own perception around what exists.

What if cleansing your mind with hopeful, joyful, positive thoughts is the rebalancing that's been long overdue, after so many years of existing solely within the most negative interpretations you could come up with?

What if, after an entire lifetime of being sold the idea that the point of your life is to exist as perfectly as possible, you could now open up to the notion that perhaps you are, instead, here to enjoy the ride while you're still on it?

THIS YEAR, LET GO *of* THE PEOPLE *who* AREN'T READY *to* LOVE YOU

It is the hardest thing you will ever have to do, and it will also be the most important: stop giving your love to those who aren't ready to love you.

Stop having hard conversations with people who don't want to change. Stop showing up for people who are indifferent about your presence. Stop prioritizing people who make you an option. Stop loving people who aren't ready to love you.

I know that your instinct is to do whatever you can to earn the good graces of everyone you can, but that is also the impulse that will rob you of your time, your energy and your sanity.

When you start showing up to your life wholly and completely, with joy and interest and commitment, not everyone is going to be ready to meet you there.

It doesn't mean you need to change who you are. It means you need to stop loving people who aren't ready to love you.

If you're left out, subtly insulted, mindlessly forgotten about, or easily disregarded by the people you spend the most time with, you're doing yourself an incredible disservice by continuing to offer your energy and life to them.

You are not for everyone, and everyone is not for you. That's what makes it so special when you do find the few people with whom you have a genuine friendship, love or relationship: you'll know how precious it is because you've experienced what it isn't.

But the longer you spend trying to force someone to love you when they aren't capable, the longer you're robbing yourself of that very connection. It is waiting for you. There are billions of people on this planet, and so many of them are going to meet you at your level, vibe where you are, connect with where you're going.

…But the longer you stay small, tucked into the familiarity of the people who use you as a cushion, a back burner option, a therapist and a ploy for their emotional labor, the longer you keep yourself out of the community you crave.

Maybe if you stop showing up, you'll be less liked.

Maybe you'll be forgotten about altogether.

Maybe if you stop trying, the relationship will cease.

Maybe if you stop texting, your phone will stay dark for days and weeks.

Maybe if you stop loving someone, the love between you will dissolve.

That doesn't mean you ruined a relationship. It means that the only thing sustaining a relationship was the energy you and you alone were putting into it.

That's not love. That's attachment.

The most precious, important thing that you have in your life is your energy. It is not your time that is limited, it is your energy. What you give it to each day is what you will create more and more of in your life. What you give your time to is what will define your existence.

When you realize this, you'll begin to understand why you're so anxious when you spend your time with people who are wrong for you, and in jobs or places or cities that are wrong, too.

You'll begin to realize that the foremost important thing you can do for your life and yourself and everyone you know is to protect your energy more fiercely than anything else.

Make your life a safe haven in which only people that have the capacity to care and listen and connect are allowed.

You are not responsible for saving people.

You are not responsible for convincing them they want to be saved.

It is not your job to show up for people and give away your life to them, little by little, moment by moment, because you pity them, because you feel bad, because you "should," because you're obligated, because, at the root of it all, you're afraid to not be liked back.

It is your job to realize that you are the master of your fate, and that you are accepting the love you think you're worthy of.

Decide you're deserving of real friendship, true commitment and complete love with people who are healthy and thriving.

Then wait in the darkness, just for a little bit…

…And watch how quickly everything begins to change.

47 WAYS *to* PRACTICE MICRO-HEALING *in* *your* EVERYDAY LIFE

01 | Do something that your future self will thank you for, even if it is small.

02 | Appreciate something you have today that your past self would be impressed by, even if it feels normal now.

03 | Start saying "thank you" for what you want as though it has already happened. Write it down, say it out loud. Even once is enough.

04 | Learn the power of momentum. Start with small tasks in the day and let it build.

05 | Make one tiny shift in the right direction. Drink one half glass of water. Walk around the block. Take one deep breath.

06 | Just for today, let yourself feel how you feel.

07 | Find a healthy, productive distraction for when your mind needs to be rerouted.

08 | Unfollow every single person who makes you feel bad about yourself.

09 | See your discomfort as your subconscious way of telling yourself that you are capable of more, and better, than you have at this current moment.

10 | **Junk journal.** Open up a notebook and scribble down exactly how you feel. Stop trying to invalidate them with positivity. That will arise on its own once your subconscious is more clear.

11 | **Let yourself dream.** Imagine what you want to build and create next in your life.

12 | Give yourself something to look forward to. Plan a trip, make a date, or take yourself out somewhere.

13 | If there is something you need to change in your life, start today. Look for new jobs. Write a letter to someone you need to apologize to. If time is not resolving the matter, then time may be waiting on you.

14 | Do not believe everything that you think.

15 | Do not trust everything that you feel.

16 | Think back on everything you worried about that turned out to be nothing, and how sometimes, our fears lead us to believe our worst thoughts are most real.

17 | Think back on all those times you had strong, overwhelming feelings that you didn't really understand and

realize that sometimes, you just had to learn how to let them pass.

18 | Do something each day that helps you get to know yourself better. Write down what you like and what you don't. Identify your values, your beliefs, your hopes, your fears.

19 | Spend time with people who understand you.

20 | Do something for someone without asking for anything in return.

21 | Don't be afraid to disengage. Spend less time on your phone, decline events that make you feel drained at the end. Remember the sacredness of your energy and attention.

22 | Read something that makes you think about the world differently.

23 | Note what comes effortlessly to you, within this is a key to your future.

24 | Note what is interesting to you, within this is a key to your purpose.

25 | Note what you struggle with the most, within this is a key to what you're here to heal.

26 | Practice standing up for yourself in a healthy way. Look in the mirror and practice setting boundaries. Learn to speak your truth with dignity and grace.

27 | Recognize that whatever bothers you most about other people can reveal the unconscious truth about yourself — use these discomforts as opportunities to heal your own invisible wounds.

28 | Lean in deeply to that which brings you joy.

29 | Do something special for the people you really care about, even if it's just a reminder text of how much they're loved.

30 | Create a vision board.

31 | Study the daily habits of people you admire.

32 | Study the daily habits of the people you do not admire.

33 | When you feel the impulse to judge another person, remind yourself gently that every time you do so, you only continue to narrow your own self-approval.

34 | State what you are feeling, in clear and honest terms. This will help you process and accept it, even if it doesn't make complete sense to you right now.

35 | Interrogate one negative thought. Instead of running on autopilot, stop and ask yourself: *Is this true? Do I know for a fact this is true? Who told me this is true?*

36 | Then ask yourself: *Does this thought help me move my life in the direction I would like it to go?*

37 | Give yourself permission to rest. If all you were able to do today was wake up and keep breathing, that's okay.

38 | Make a to-do list, then cut it in half. Then cut it in half again. You should be left with the one or two most imperative tasks. Focus on those and only those. Go from there.

39 | Meditate on how far you've come. Make a list of all the things you have, do, and feel that you never imagined would be possible.

40 | Meditate on how much you've overcome. Consider everything that happened in the past that you swore you'd never get over, and note that you always did.

41 | Express genuine gratitude. Find something you are actually happy to have.

42 | If feeling good is too far from where you're at, just try to feel neutral.

43 | Sleep when you are tired.

44 | Eat when you are hungry.

45 | Pause before you react. You are allowed to be angry, but you will want to be mindful of allowing that feeling to make you take action that could impact your safety or quality of life for years to come.

46 | Write yourself a note in which you outline exactly what to do when you have a panicky feeling. When you're thinking clearly, tell yourself what to do when you're not.

47 | **Remember that you're mortal.** All of this will pass. No time is guaranteed. You are not stuck forever. Life moves quickly and it does not stop. You are only here for a moment. Try to savor it as much as you can.

THE TRUTH *of who* YOU ARE *is more* THAN YOU *let* YOURSELF BELIEVE

Infinite versions of you exist.

There's the person you were yesterday and the person you are today. There's the person you were five years ago and the person you will be in another ten. There's the person you were this morning and then the person you'll be tonight.

There's the person that exists within the minds of each person you know and meet and come across and love. Every single one of them has a unique image of you in their minds, informed by their own experiences and preferences and beliefs and feelings they have about their own selves.

When we feel most stuck, it is often because we are trying to decipher who we really are by piecing together images we assume others have of us. What we don't realize is that there is not just one, singular version of us that exists. There's our experience of ourselves, and then the kaleidoscope of ways we are perceived by others. When we spend all of our lives trying to manage those perceptions, we become completely lost within them.

What if there's a bigger truth here, one that's begging to be seen?

You have probably had more experiences than you can remember, and they were better than you can recall. You've seen more of the world than you realize. You've felt more happiness than you are generally conscious of, you've known more joy, felt more inspiration, and have succeeded more times than you are aware of when you're in your most doubtful moments.

You've been more accepted than you remember—more appreciated, and validated than you know. More people saw your potential than you realize. They liked you more than you believe. You were more wanted than you think—by friends, by family, by potential lovers who longed for you in ways you probably never would have imagined in the first place.

When the people closest to you look at you, they see far more of your greatness than you ever would looking at yourself.

You've made a bigger impact on the world than you realize. There are more hearts you have soothed in moments of grief, more minds you have inspired to see hope where there was once defeat. There have been more instances where one kind, selfless act cascaded a ripple effect across the entire world. Your love has touched people on the other side of the planet, you just don't know it right now.

You have more going for you than you understand right now.

It's easy to define ourselves by the empty spaces, the ways in which we lack. And yet those are not always gaps within us waiting to be filled, rather, the simple contrast between all we are and all we were never meant to be. When we can learn to hold space for all the coexisting truths of our lives we can begin to understand that experience itself is both contraction and expansion.

The high and low of it, the beautiful and heartbreaking altogether.

We are not summarized or defined by any one instance or experience. The static, singular image we think others have of us in their minds—it's usually a projection of our greatest hopes and deepest fears. We are fluid, evolving beings. We are different from one moment to the next. We spend so much time making assumptions about how we are in the world instead of actually feeling into our lived experience. We allow ourselves to become labelled and defined by what we think we've done and how others have responded to it, rather than who we are going to become and whether or not we can be at peace with it.

When we show up to each day as a different person, the world will start to shift to perceive us that way.

We are in no way forever limited, or permanently defined by who we were in the past.

But you, more than anyone, are most inclined to see yourself that way. You, more than anyone, are most inclined to believe that the worst things about you are the most true things about you.

Nobody—not one single person alive—is thinking about you more than you are thinking about yourself.

They are too busy thinking about their own lives, and how they're perceived, and whether they are enough, and on and on.

As we begin to heal, we start to recognize that our lives do not have to be defined by how we think we are seen.

The truth is that to some people, you are the beauty standard. To others, you are simply overlooked. To some, you are a genius at your craft. To others, you are irrelevant. To some, you are an incredible friend. To others, you are a complete stranger. To some, you are a life partner. To others, you are not someone they'd even date. To some, you are a teacher. To others, you are a student. To some, you are a guide. To others, you are a beginner. To some, you are a shining light. To others, you reveal their darkness.

The reality is that you exist in so many different forms and images and beliefs and stories—and yet, the only one that is ever really going to matter is the one you tell yourself.

Allow this knowing to free you.

Allow it to help you see that there is more dimension, more contrast, more nuance, and more goodness within you than you have ever allowed yourself to believe.

You have done more, seen more, and meant more to others than you could ever know.

Close this book for a moment.

Take one second just to breathe and look around.

There is more here than you would ever realize.

There is more waiting than you would ever assume.

THIS *is* HOW *to* START OVER, *even if* YOU'RE STAYING RIGHT *where* YOU ARE

When it's time to start over, you won't know you're at the start of a new beginning, because all it will feel like is an overwhelming end.

All of a sudden, and possibly out of nowhere, something you've known has come to a halt. It's likely that this thing was something you were deeply attached to, hopeful about, or invested in, because our lives are shifting and adapting all of the time, and the only instances in which we don't move with them are when we're too stuck to see another way forward.

It will feel, for a moment, as though the world is crashing in on you.

The resounding feeling that you'll experience is one of total defeat. You'll wonder what's next, and how you will ever possibly go on. Right now, you're able to measure what you're going to lose, but not what you're going to gain.

And that's if you're lucky.

For most of us, we don't even realize that we have to let go, only that what we're doing now is not working.

Even if it seems like the "rug was pulled out from under you," it wasn't. This thing most likely hadn't been working for a long time, and you were in denial. Your delusions and dreams about how it would transform into something you want it to be are just that—unreal. It's time to get out of that and into reality, into the now, into your actual life.

That is what it means to start over.

It means that it's time to reconcile what we've known wasn't working all along, what those things were acting as a bandaid for. When we're too attached to the outcome of something, and we have little tolerance for its presence changing whatsoever, it's usually because we are using that thing to hide something about ourselves, and that something is our dissatisfaction.

Maybe a relationship ended and you cannot imagine how you'll date again.

Maybe you've realized a career path isn't viable and you cannot imagine how you'll ever make money in the future.

Maybe you're finally accepting that you know you need to move, but the idea of establishing yourself in a new place with new people seems too daunting to even try.

Deep down, the relationship that ended was a distraction from the relationship you don't have with yourself. The career path that didn't pan out was never viable, you were just unwilling to try something outside of your comfort zone, and nothing new is within it. The place you need to leave might have been right for a while, but you've outgrown it, and your life is no longer supporting the person you want to be or the place you want to go.

You will have to spend many nights by yourself, in candle-light, making yourself dinner, learning to love yourself, to be alone with yourself and enjoy that time. You will have to stay precisely where you are and learn to mend the wound of your unworthiness before you can be loved.

You will have to go back to the starting point of your job, and work with what you have and what you've done. Remember what you're good at, what you're experienced in, what you feel called to. The intersection of those things are your path, and your path is right in front of you, even if another option is more appealing.

You will have to build a home no matter where you are. You will have to decorate and settle and reach out. You will have to find rhythms and routines. You will have to be vulnerable, and you will have to be seen.

There is nowhere we can turn to that is an escape from ourselves.

It's time to start over, and it's time to begin right here.

Weed out what's dead in your life.

Nourish the garden around your soul.

Start where you are and with what you have.

Stand on what you've built.

Close the gaps in your own foundation.

Strengthen what already exists.

Deepen your roots and spread your branches wide.

Then see how you feel.

We cannot keep running in circles and expect our lives to blossom, we have to stay where we are and have the courage to heal what's broken within us before turning to yet another outside source to mend the damage.

When we live like this, we exist in a constant state of running from ourselves.

We can start over right where we are, because at any time, we can change the way we see ourselves and our lives, and that's all healing is, anyway.

It's realizing that your inner love is inherent to you and always has been, it's just been buried behind doubt.

It's realizing that your path forward is innate to you and always has been, it's just been hiding behind denial.

It's realizing that the place you're supposed to be is right where you are now, even if it's not where you'll be forever.

We heal when we learn how to adjust how we show up, not how we change what we show up to.

Our lives are very often a reflection, and extension, of ourselves. We can run to the ends of the earth and still not feel whole because what we were looking for was a reinvention of the way we see, what we perceive, and how we feel.

That's work that starts right here, and right now.

No matter where your life takes you, you are always with you—until the very end.

Nobody else can save you from yourself.

The point was never that you adjusted everything around you until it was made perfect, but that you adjusted the way you see everything until you realize that it is enough, and it always has been.

the GREATEST HEALING *often* HAPPENS *in the* *most* ORDINARY WAYS

When you begin your healing journey, you will be searching for epiphanies. Life-changing, soul-opening, mind-bending truths. Drastic changes, rapid uprooting, the fierce releasing of what you can no longer stand and the obsessive need to find something that makes you feel a little better, even just for a moment.

One of the most subtle challenges will be that the thick of it often happens in the most ordinary ways.

It's about setting an intention to heal. Writing it down on a piece of paper somewhere you see often. Realizing that nobody knows what to do at the beginning, so sometimes the most powerful way we can begin is by making a statement to the universe about what we're going to do.

It's about carving out space for deep rest. The deepest rest you've ever given yourself. It's about realizing that your body knows what to do, and your job is to support it, to step out of the way.

It's about changing your environment, both in big ways and small. This might mean moving. It might mean cleansing your space of relics, so you are no longer living in a museum of the past. It's about realizing that you will adapt to what's around you, and so you must choose wisely. You must create even just one corner of peace within your own little world, recognizing finally that "home" was never a place that existed anywhere outside of your own heart.

It's about doing the practical things, the budgeting and the blood tests. The doctor's appointments and the making of plans. The calendars and the emails. The supplements and the exercise routines, however simple they may be at first. These things are often the first to be cast aside when we are hurting, and yet they are also the most vital.

It's about finding the kind of support that's right for you—the trainer, the therapist, the life coach—whatever is needed for your own unique journey.

It's about rediscovering the little joys of life—the long baths, the page-turning novels, the quiet Saturday mornings, the clean sheets, the stars, the city lights, the ocean—and realizing that they were the big things all along.

It's about affirming what you want to be true, and knowing, somewhere deep down, that it already is. It's about visualizing your future self and being willing to believe that maybe, just maybe, that person could be real. It's about standing up for yourself when it's necessary, and recognizing all of the times when you're misinterpreting a mindless comment as a slight. These things all require deeper levels of self-awareness, evaluation, and consciousness.

It's about recognizing that the heat of your trauma is trying to prevent you from living your life. Somewhere, deep down, you know that when you go out and try to make your way in the world, everything goes wrong. So your fear is trying to lock you down, and it's trying to keep you safe.

What it does not know is that there is no greater failure than a life unlived.

There is no greater pain than having your heart go unloved, your soul go unseen.

It's about choosing not to give your mental attention and emotional energy to things that will not grow into experiences you want to be having. It's about realizing that you can construct a new dream. It's about releasing who you are, in the smallest ways, and realizing that sometimes, the most ordinary things are the most defining, the most saving, the most soothing, the most important, the most overlooked, and the most real.

THE *8* PHASES *of* *deep* PERSONAL TRANSFORMATION

Positive change is often planted through seeds that can sometimes make us feel more uncertain, fearful, and anxious than anything else.

This is because we often don't think to change our lives until change is the only option we have.

We are hardwired for homeostasis.

We are designed to remain in comfort, which is just familiarity.

But this isn't always what's best for us, and deep down, we know that at some level. We often find that when we do not heed our own intuitive nudges, life tends to present us with circumstances that make us move forward regardless.

Instead of fearing this process, we should learn to honor it, because it means that something greater is often waiting for us on the other side.

These are the 8 things that happen right before your life changes for the better.

01 | A catalytic event occurs.

Sometimes it's massive, sometimes, it's subtle.

For many people, the catalyst that prompts them to begin a process of positive disintegration is often the loss of a major relationship, job, or family member. In one way or another, something that you expected to be around for the foreseeable future was taken, and in that, your sense of safety was removed as well.

Other times, this event can be much harder to detect. In fact, you may not realize that anything has happened at all.

Instead, what's been planted is a seed of doubt. Maybe you saw an old friend and it prompted you to evaluate your progress in life. Maybe someone close to you is moving on with their life in a big way and it's made you rethink what you really want. Maybe your stress and dissatisfaction have simply just started to compile and you find yourself wondering how much longer you can sustain your current routine.

Regardless, life almost never changes for the better unless a disruptor is present—something that makes us question, and dare to change, our own status quo.

02 | You're forced out of denial.

The thing about things we lose is that they weren't working for a very long time, we just didn't realize it.

With the exception of an abrupt and sudden loss of someone you love or the closure of a company you assumed would be around forever, for example, almost anything we lose in life has often been foreshadowed for a very long time.

That relationship that ended? It wasn't working for a long time, that's why it's over. That job that you abruptly left? It wasn't working for a long time, that's why you quit. That lifestyle you were desperate to keep up with? It wasn't you, which is why you couldn't sustain it.

It's really hard to accept this, but so important to acknowledge: almost nothing in life leaves us without purpose.

It's only a matter of when we accept this truth.

03 | You feel swells of anger and fear.

In the aftermath of the loss, you often find yourself going through the grieving process, even if you didn't actually lose a loved one.

All of these emotions are extremely valid.

It is healthy and normal to feel anger when a boundary has been crossed or you are facing some sort of injustice. It is healthy and normal to feel sad and scared when life abruptly changes and you're not sure what's next.

The longer you resist these emotions, the longer they linger.

They are part of the process of great change and offer within them the seeds of more profound wisdom to come.

04 | You begin processing old emotions and memories.

Before you know it, this seed has sprouted into a thousand other spirals, all of which have left you questioning all that you are, and all that you once hoped to be.

This did not create these fears and feelings, it revealed them.

Everything that you were clasping so tightly to was a way in which you were shielding yourself from these emotions, many of which you'd buried so deep inside, you assumed they were gone forever.

Emotions often remain within us until they tell us what it is we need to know.

That message is not that we are worthless and unlovable, as they may often feel. Instead, the message is usually that we are not holding ourselves within life circumstances that fully honor our worth, and we are not acknowledging just how loved we truly are, and therefore, we aren't seeking relationships in which we feel and see that truth reflected at us.

In this process of simply remembering what had hurt you in the past and how you felt about it, you will likely realize that a lot of your self-belief was created by experiences that compounded upon one another, and now, you're giving yourself the chance to unpack.

You'll have a lighter load to bear on the other side.

05 | You get a glimpse of a better path.

Usually, towards the end of the unraveling process, right about when you feel like giving up for good, you will probably get a peek at the light at the end of the tunnel.

Maybe one day, out of nowhere, you come up with a novel idea, maybe you happen to connect with someone who happens to have a job offer that would be perfect for you, maybe you're prompted to start the business you had been thinking about, maybe you meet someone, maybe you move, maybe you get the feeling that any one of those things is in your immediate future.

In one way or another, you start to get the sneaking suspicion that there might just be something really good around the corner, but at this point, you probably don't quite believe it. That's okay, you don't have to.

All you have to do is keep stepping forward.

06 | You start making small adjustments.

With those new visions in mind, you start making small changes.

Maybe all of your processing and discomfort has prompted you to change the way you style your hair or approach your work, or what you do with your spare time. Little by little, you start adapting to your newly emerging self. You find new truths, new staples, and new routines, ones that suit the person you're becoming, not the person you've been.

07 | You take a big leap.

Finally, those adjustments start adding up to something, and you know it's time to leap forward.

This might be actually starting the new job or leaving the old one, moving, or changing something else about your life that once felt completely unmovable.

This part of the process is vital because it's the scariest, and also the most important.

To truly usher in new and positive things in your life, you often have to reach for them. This means that you have to step out of your comfort zone, think and act in ways you never have, and believe in yourself and your vision more than you've ever believed in anything else.

This is the leap that the beginning of the process was preparing you for.

This was the dream that was hiding deep within you, the one that was nudging you to let go of what you had before, to address the feelings that were blocking your vision and your flow, and the one that is finally ready to become reality.

This has existed within you all along.

It's been waiting for you this entire time.

You just had to find the courage to choose it, and sometimes, that means not giving yourself any other choice.

08 | You see the purpose in the pain.

Finally, you're past the breakthrough, and into your new life.

If you're one of the very lucky ones, you've made it far enough to understand that there was a purpose in all of this, especially the uncomfortable moments.

If you're aware enough, you might realize that had you not originally been so uncomfortable, you might have gone through the rest of your life with unrealized dreams, holding yourself back out of small and irrational fears, and living half the life you were destined to, all because you didn't have the courage to change.

Sometimes, when we don't step effortlessly toward what it is we're meant to be doing, we create circumstances for ourselves that make it impossible to do anything but move forward.

Destiny cannot be denied.

Perhaps, in this, you might find some peace.

Maybe you will realize that your emotions are nothing to be afraid of, because the storm often clears the skies and waters the seeds for the life you had been asking for, dreaming of, and planning to actually live all along.

You just needed a nudge.

7 PSYCHOLOGICAL BIASES *that are* MAKING *you* RESIST *your* OWN GROWTH

Growth is hard.

Sometimes, it's downright terrifying.

It requires us to take an honest look at ourselves, to abandon what we've known, and to suspend ourselves in uncertainty without knowing when we'll ever find the next step.

What this means is that we will remain what we have always been unless we consciously choose to become something else. Sure, everyone evolves and adapts over time, but if you aren't intentional about it, you'll end up the product of who and what is around you as opposed to an authentic expression of who *you* really are.

Growth is a required assignment.

The only question is *when* we do it, and how long it takes for us to realize that we often have to defy some of our instincts in order to create a better reality for ourselves.

Here are a few of those unconscious fears that prevent us from becoming all that we possibly can be, and how they might specifically be affecting you.

01 | You have become comfortable being uncomfortable.

In the same way that too much of a decadent dessert can overwhelm the taste buds and become unappealing, we reject intense emotional highs when we aren't used to them.

Gay Hendricks, author of *The Big Leap,* calls this hitting this your "upper limit."

His theory is that people have a predisposed tolerance for happiness, and when our emotions exceed that limit, we begin to unconsciously self-sabotage in order to bring ourselves back to a more comfortable baseline.

Any change, no matter how positive, will be uncomfortable until it is also familiar.

Any time you're looking to make a significant positive change in your life, a mindset shift must accompany it. If you don't believe you deserve to feel good, you'll limit your capacity for experiencing good things. If you're not used to life being easy, you'll make it hard to anchor yourself back down to what you're familiar with.

Overcoming this is not a matter of overwhelming your system with positivity.

It's actually a process of grounding yourself, expressing gratitude, and shifting your belief system to reflect the idea that you are allowed to feel good, you are allowed to create goodness in your life, and you deserve the beautiful things that are blossoming—you don't need to keep uprooting them.

02 | You don't know all your options yet.

The human mind cannot accurately predict what it hasn't yet known.

When you imagine a potential outcome for your life, what you're really envisioning is a solution to a past experience, a feeling you've had before and would like to maintain. What you cannot account for are the things that you wouldn't think to ask for, because you don't know that you want them.

Real growth requires genuine exploration, a period of trial and error. It requires you to first admit that you might not know what you want.

This uncertainty is an unnerving experience, so most people avoid it completely. They numb out their fear of the unknown with mind-consuming activities, failing to realize that without allowing oneself to accept the unknown, the answers will always remain at bay. Instead of trying to construct an experience of happiness, we can find it in the moment if we're gearing our mindset to appreciating what we already have instead of planning how to acquire what we don't.

Through this, we inch closer to what it is that actually makes us feel best, not what appears best or "should" be right from the outside looking in.

03 | You believe that negative potential outcomes are more likely than the positive ones.

When you imagine all of the possible outcomes for your life, the negative options probably seem more real than the positive ones. This is because of negativity bias, which is where we are inclined to believe that bad things are more real than good things, because we're more afraid of them.

Because one appears as a threat and the other doesn't, our attention naturally gravitates toward what we feel we need to be more aware of. However, it has the opposite effect of self-defense. When we believe too much in our negativity biases, we end up resisting change, taking fewer chances, and overall adjusting to a less optimistic outlook on life.

Negativity bias limits us not because we aren't able to be realistic, but because we don't understand that positive outcomes are often *more likely* than worst case scenarios, they just aren't as emotionally triggering.

04 | You're staying loyal to what you've put a lot of time into, even if it's not what's really right for you long-term.

You're most inclined to stick to what you've invested in the most, even if it's unviable long-term, and even if a better opportunity is presenting itself.

This is because of sinking cost fallacy.

What this bias prevents us from seeing is that *the ship is sinking anyway,* and every additional ounce of effort, time or resource that we put into it is yet another bit that we lose. We can't salvage it just because we've spent so much time believing in it. Sometimes, even the things we've given everything to are just not what's best for us long-term.

It's hard to let go, but it's harder not to.

05 | You are giving precedence to what you believed first.

The brain tends to prioritize and overvalue whatever it is that we did, knew, saw or learned first.

This makes it hard for us to change course.

Your very first approach and assessment of your career prospects are anchoring what you believe is possible today. Your very first introduction to certain geographical areas or types of people is likely the same way.

Whatever you were exposed to first or believed in first is going to take precedence in your mind. It's important that you're aware of this, because when a better option presents itself, you have to be able to see it for what it is.

06 | You're making a long-term assessment based on a short-term experience.

When you declare that you'll never find love because you just went through a breakup, or consider yourself fundamentally awful looking because you're not loving your outfit today, or you're sinking in the feeling that you'll never find your way in life because you feel lost right now, what you're doing is extrapolating.

Extrapolation is the projection of a single experience into a long-term assumption about life.

"This moment is not your life, this is a moment in your life."—Ryan Holiday

What you're not realizing is that just because you're temporarily having a negative experience does not mean that it will define the rest of your life in the way that you fear it will.

What you're really saying is that you can't see a way out of your current circumstances because in some way, *you don't completely control them.*

Instead of trying to form a definitive statement about how life is or isn't or will or won't be based on your temporary circumstances, try to see them for what they really are: an experience you're having currently, that will eventually fade out, as all others do.

07 | You're using self-reflection as an escape mechanism, rather than a way to actually change your life.

When we begin something new in our lives, it's almost always because we have a revelation about it, or ourselves.

We realize that we need to course-correct, we have an "aha!" moment about the people we want to be, we let go of what's holding us back, we find courage, and we embark upon our new path.

This is often where people find themselves in a slump.

While many people think the process of releasing the past and embracing the future is scary, it's also very freeing. So freeing, in fact, that the high of having epiphanies and life-changing realizations can sometimes eclipse the actual implementation of them.

The honest truth is that no matter what you choose to do or be in life, to do it well and long-term, everything will become boring and monotonous at some point or another. That's sometimes the reality of life. While you'll undoubtedly feel more peace and fulfillment pursuing what's really right for you, you're going to have down days, you're going to have periods of burnout, you're going to have moments of second guessing yourself, and you're absolutely going to realize that it's often far more exciting and thrilling to decide to totally uproot and start again than it is to simply stick with the path day-in and day-out.

EVERYTHING *that's* TRULY RIGHT *for you* WILL *make you* FEEL AT PEACE

Everything that is meant for you will feel like a deep exhale, as though you are returning home to a place you forgot existed. We so often yearn for and want the things that help us escape who we are, but the things that are actually meant for us—the ones that arrive and stay—they make us feel a sense of steady calm. We do not need to be swept off our feet, but grounded through them. In the moment is where love really exists. The moment is the only place we can come alive.

Everything that is truly right for you will make you feel at ease.

Everything that is truly right for you will seem so simple, so obvious, so comfortable.

Everything that is truly right for you will choose you as quickly as you choose it.

Everything that is truly right for you will happen serendipitously and spontaneously. It will come to you when you expect it and when you don't, as both a surprise and a certainty. It will seem like such an obvious fact of your life and yet entirely new, all at once.

We often come to believe that the things that are most right for us are the ones that give us the biggest emotions, and that is a mistake. The things that are truly right for us give us the *deepest* emotions. Love is a pervasive, steady presence, not a heart-pumping dash of lust. Destiny is a subtle coincidence, it makes you stop and say, well, *isn't it funny how that worked out.*

What's right for us isn't a harsh declaration, it isn't something we have to force or wonder about for too long. It isn't something that leaves us looking for signs, it doesn't require us to poll our friends to gather their opinions. It doesn't leave us questioning, grieving, self-doubting. It doesn't put us on hold. It doesn't feel as though we have to grab it before it is gone, but rather, that it will always be waiting for us when we are ready.

The things that are most right for us are also the easiest to miss, because they are often subtle at first.

Little things become big things over time, we just have to give them a chance. We just have to stay the course. We just have to realize that life will magnetize to us what is meant to be ours.

Sometimes, our only job is to step out of the way.

I know how hard it is to believe that the right things will find you in a world where they so often haven't. In a life where you've felt so deeply disappointed and disillusioned, it will sometimes take every ounce of faith you can muster to believe that there is, indeed, a greater path.

Sometimes, you won't believe in it at all.

That's okay.

The right things will find you in the exact same way that everything else has. Everything that's ever come and everything that ever will—it was brought to life by your presence and your participation. The right things don't often have to be chased, but rather, pursued. They don't have to be convinced to stay, but rather, committed to. They are not things we discover one day, but inklings that are offered to us, instances of opportunity upon which we begin to build our lives.

When we go out looking for our soulmate relationships, we are often discouraged to find a sea of fellow human beings, all broken and lost in their own ways. Slowly, we discover that the people who are most meant for us are not only the ones with whom we have an instant, electric connection, but also the ones with whom we can grow with, walk with, evolve with. The roots of great love stories are planted slowly over the years, with each turn you take together, each lesson learned. The love you desire is one you create with someone who is as equally willing to expand with you as you are with them. We do not lose love when we lack passion, we lose it when we lack any further potential for growth.

When we go out looking for our dream jobs, our life purpose, we are often discouraged to find that every path presents a mountain of challenges, and through the process, every one of our fears about our potential unworthiness comes to the forefront. We mistakenly believed that pursuing our dreams would be something that helped us escape from being so human, when it is, in fact, the very way we become most human of all. What we are looking for is not a life path that is easy, but one that is worthwhile. One that we are willing to hurt for, to reach for, to stretch for. One where the difficulty doesn't become a deterrent, but a subtle motivator. One where we can go home at the end of the night and close our eyes and feel at ease with the fact that we tried our best toward something that really mattered in our lives or in someone else's, and that, itself, is enough.

When we wake up each day and wonder how we might design an existence that honors and reveals the deepest layers of who we really are, we are often fraught to realize that no matter how much conscious intention we infuse into our days, there are always variables, always the world beyond us, raging beyond our control. What we are looking for is not a way to convince ourselves that our bubble of serenity is all that exists, but to create our own personal safe haven as a constant reminder that it is possible to make a beautiful way within this world, it is possible to return home to yourself.

The things that are truly right for you will make you feel at ease, and not because they are simple, or easy, or perfect right away. They will make you feel peace because you know that you are meant for them, for better or for worse. They will make you feel peace because you will end each day knowing you gave your all toward something that mattered to you. They will make you feel at peace because you will quickly realize that within this whole huge universe, to have one soul in front of you, one task that is uniquely yours, one body through which a temporary breath sustains you, is an improbable miracle that you are living through.

The things that are truly right for you will find you, and they will stay. They will grow you, challenge you, and change you.

Most of all, they will not exist in the distance, in the future, in a potential version of reality.

It is their undeniable presence that will ultimately put your heart at ease.

YOU *have to* PRACTICE LETTING GO

Almost every last one of us lives with the assumption that if something is not right for us, it will simply be pulled away in time. We linger, we wonder, we grasp onto what's so clearly not a match and we wait for the universe to do the dirty work—and feel devastated once it's done.

We think of letting go as a last ditch effort to our own progress and sanity—we will let go only if we have to, only if we are forced, only if the world truly proves to us that something is not meant to be.

There is an easier way.

Letting go is not an event, it is a practice.

It is something we learn to do with the small stuff, so when the big stuff comes around, we know how.

We have to learn to let go of thoughts, of moments.

We have to learn to let go of acquaintances, care for others' opinions, so many petty arguments and fights we can choose not to pick. We have to learn to let go of the items that serve only as relics of a time that has passed, the clothes that dressed the people we no longer are. We have to learn to let go of the dreams we chose for the people we eventually outgrew, we have to learn to let go of the idea that other people are meant to live up to our expectations of them, rather than their own unpredictable truths.

We have made the process of letting go seem like this superhuman feat only attainable for the truly enlightened. We find so many ways around it. Revenge bodies, gaining closure, proving them wrong. We find so many ways to at once make it seem as though we have moved on completely, and yet remain precisely where we used to be—living through the gaze of what we imagine someone else might see.

Letting go is as effortless as an exhale.

You do it all the time.

There are so many thousands of things you have released, and only a few that you're still clinging to.

Sometimes, letting go is an action, sometimes, it is a decision, and very often, it is a matter of distraction. We let go not when we think we are supposed to, but when our minds move onto reciting different stories, building new realities. We move on not when we have adequately picked apart the pieces of what used to be, but when we begin to think more about what we'd like to build in its place.

We aren't really letting go.

We are just accepting what's already gone.

What we are actually releasing is just an idea.

An idea we had about who we were, or who someone else could be. An idea we had about how the future would unfold, and how we would arrive into it. An idea we had about the world, and how it works, and whether or not we are safe.

You see, letting go is not a process of simply releasing into nothingness. It is a process of profound growth. In place of what no longer serves, we are forced to reach for what will finally heal.

THIS *is* HOW YOU FIND *the* CONFIDENCE *to* PURSUE *what* YOU *really* LOVE

This is for every person who finds themselves staring wide-eyed at the prospect of their dreams while their chest sinks as they become overwhelmed with doubt, with dread, with fear that this feeling might be a sign not to move forward.

This is for every person whose thoughts are imagined echoes of what the world might say, all of which ultimately circles back to the same sentiment.

Who are you to do this?

Maybe you're young and you're learning. Maybe you're not-so-young and you have an established career that's a safe bet to a fast and easy retirement. Maybe you're switching fields entirely. Maybe you're trying something completely new. Maybe you're finally getting the courage to share what you've been creating and dreaming of since you were doing it alone in your childhood bedroom.

No matter where these words may find you on your journey, they are for you if there is something deep within you calling you to your future, and an overwhelming doubt trying to keep you stuck right where you are.

You need to look around.

Not at the greats, not at your idols.

Comparing yourself to them will only ever make you feel small and unworthy. Instead of measuring yourself by this standard, consider their successes proof of what's possible, and then look beside you. Watch your peers. See what those around you are doing. Notice how many artists are creating and building businesses born of their passions. Watch how many writers are crafting poems, how many coaches are leading their clients, how many classes are selling, how education is moving, how art is being purchased and displayed.

The world we live in today makes things possible that were *completely impossible* just a few years ago.

People want to support you.

They want to learn from you.

They want to grow with you.

You are part of this ecosystem, you already fit in.

If you watch those beside you for long enough, what you'll notice is that those who are steadfast in the life of their deepest longing aren't necessarily the most gifted, the most outrageously talented, or the most perfect at their craft. What they are is just a few steps ahead of you, because they showed up consistently during the time you spent wondering if you should.

When we are *too good* at something, our practice of it often devolves into mania and madness. We become consumed with it. Our sense of importance eclipses the work itself, and we render ourselves paralyzed.

You don't need to be this way.

It doesn't have to look like this.

Those idols you're in the shadows of? They had day jobs.

The people who lived long, fulfilling lives pursuing what they truly loved didn't always make their income from it, or even a lot of money from it. Others did, and do. Either way, you don't need to measure your worthiness as an artist or creator or entrepreneur or seeker by the level at which your commitment overshadows all else.

Showing up is what makes your work worthwhile.

Showing up is what creates your worth.

Showing up and *allowing* is what makes your best product.

It is not comparisons of expertise, it is not complexity or realism, it is not who has the hottest, quickest take. It is not who is successful fastest, or who is most front-facing about it. It is not about the few people who can create absolute masterpieces of their work and their lives, but the many who are willing to show up and do the best they can—create what inspires them and makes them feel and think—who prove that often, what we want to share and consume is more about what resonates on a human level than what's so impressive, it becomes compelling.

The art on walls of museums is without question extraordinary, but it isn't often on the walls of homes—and it's not because of the price, because one could get a print, or a similar edition.

What's on the walls of homes are the messages that speak to us. That's what's on people's bookshelves, that's what's in their reading queue, that's what they share with those they love. That's what they choose to purchase, that's what they choose to engage with.

You do not have to be a fine artist to be worth pursuing what you love.

You do not need to be a bestselling author, you don't need to be on television, you don't need to be a household name, you don't need to write the next novel that's studied in classrooms around the country. You do not need to be the most impressive, elusive, untouchable.

You do not need a huge audience.

You do not need a lot of people to believe in your ability.

All you need is the willingness to create something that is authentic and true and moving to you, something that lifts you out of your human experience and into another, something that makes sense of the past, clears your perception of the future, makes you experience the same emotions you did when you first fell in love or learned to let go or felt completely at awe or inspired or at peace.

That is what should arrive into the hands of our fellow human beings.

If you are looking for permission to do what you love, if you are seeking the confidence to pursue what you would like to spend your days doing, what you are really asking for is whether or not you are good enough to be worth people's time.

So know this.

People want to hear stories that sound like their own.

They want to read work that meets them precisely where they are.

They want to collect and consume that which makes them feel understood.

They want to see outside of them a little piece of what's within them, and the only way you can create that for other people is to pull out a sliver of your soul, and put it on paper.

That's all.

It's easy to buy into the idea that what we were exposed to as "good" growing up and in school is the entirety of what goodness is. That "good" is typically defined by a very specific (and archaic) measure. It is also handpicked by those who probably have an agenda.

It is not comprehensive.

It is not representative.

It usually doesn't speak to people the way it might have 100 years ago.

The art we need today is different because we don't need to create in order to prove something about our talent anymore. Instead, we can create to share energy. We can create to express experience. We can create to make people feel heard and understood.

We can create to heal ourselves, and extend that healing outward.

If you are looking for a sign, looking for something to convince you that you are enough for your own destiny—you will have to start with the first emboldening thing, which is to feel your life from the inside instead of perceiving it from the outside.

You will have to start to deconstruct the way you have lived prior to this moment, because if you're like most people, the majority of what you do and choose and believe is your own vision is actually a copy of someone else's, a means to an end, and the end is always connection.

You will have to decide that living in accordance with your innermost truth is your top priority, for which anything can be risked and everything must. You will have to decide the extent to which you are willing to meet your soul at the mountaintop, how far you will climb and how much you will care and how deeply you will commit to the work, because *this is work.*

You will have to say goodbye to certainties.

Five year plans, regular paychecks, easy explanations about what you do.

The things that make people feel less fear, but not more alive.

You will have to draft a vision for what you could see your life becoming. You will need to be ambitious, because if you're going to go for it, you need to go all the way. While you're doing this, you will need to remove any pieces of that vision that are contingent upon trying to prove your worth to someone who might want to work with you. Your worth is your own to share, and for the world to see—no more playing mind games with yourself.

You will have to become a perpetual student.

You will have to learn about business, even if you're an artist.

You will have to learn about art, even if you are a business owner.

You will have to determine where to create your platform, how to weave together your community, where your presence would be most impactful, and how. You will have to figure out the ecosystem that will become your life, the ways in which you will create and share and then allow your work to ripple outward and into infinitely more.

You will have to start where you are.

You will have to be humbled.

You will have to stop knocking at the door and build your own hallway.

You will have to test and try to change things.

Your first approach won't be your last.

You will have to be willing to throw spaghetti at the wall more times than you think you should. You will have to be willing to fold not because something isn't working, but because something else could work better.

You will have to reinvent your self-image.

You will have to become the kind of person who makes a living doing what they love, not an amateur trying to see if they could maybe get by.

You will have to stop asking for permission.

You will have to stop thinking one person's perspective of you is the sum of who you are.

You will have to show up—again, and again, and again.

You will have to create—again, and again, and again.

Then you will have to watch for what arrives, and what remains.

Watch for what works.

Wait for what is effortless.

Keep going until you get to a point where the slightest bit of your effort reaps a large reward, and then keep going.

Keep going.

You are going to have to do things that other people are unwilling to do.

You are going to have to stop being afraid of fluctuating income or credit card debt or bad reviews or looking dumb or staying cool and pretending like you don't care.

You are going to have to care.

You are going to have to believe in your vision until someone else does.

You will have to hold a torch for yourself first.

You will have to learn that we do not spontaneously find the courage to pursue what we love one day. We sense an urge, a hunch, a small desire to take one step in the direction of our dreams. Then we keep going, even in the face of doubt and speculation. Then we pursue, with wild, open hearts, with total abandon, with complete commitment.

The confidence you are looking for will not arrive until you begin.

It will not come from mental gymnastics, comparisons, or delusions about your importance.

It will come from the simple virtue of being someone who is willing to risk it all in order to live a life that feels most true to them, to create something that they care about, and hope someone else might care about it, too.

That's all.

That's the story for all of us, every last one.

You don't need to find confidence to pursue what you really love.

You just have to be willing to start.

Then you will also need to be willing to stop.

Overcorrecting is the opposite of creativity.

Overworking is not aspirational, it's an escape mechanism.

What nobody tells you is that passion and obsession are entryways to one another. You will walk a fine line every day.

What nobody tells you is that doing what you love heightens your sensitivity to your work in a way that you are always a bit in denial of. Disapproval hurts in a soul-clenching kind of way, because you care, even if it's hard to admit you care. You care because this is more than a job. You care because this is more than just a means to an end.

These are your most vulnerable pieces.

This is who you *are.*

What nobody tells you is that doing what you love almost always means doing a lot of other stuff to pay the bills so that you can carve out space and buy back time to create freely and with abandon and in perfect alignment with what you want to become.

What nobody tells you about doing what you love is that uncertainty holds more people back than talent (or lack thereof) ever could.

What nobody tells you is that consistency outpaces talent.

What nobody tells you is that when you marry the two together—doing what comes effortlessly as often as you can—you hit your stride.

What nobody tells you is that *security is an illusion,* one that most people have bought into. There are no safe jobs, paths, choices, and if there were, *pursuing your dreams and having multiple forms of income would probably be "safer" anyway.* They don't teach you that part in school.

What nobody tells you about doing what you love is that you have to learn where to source your creativity from, because where most people begin is with their deepest pain, and where they end is in burn out.

What nobody tells you is that you will have to strengthen your creative muscle to the point that you can both work but remain relatively detached.

What nobody tells you is that it's the attachment that hurts. It's the expectation of what it should be or would be and by when.

Because for all of the unknowns, for all of the vulnerability, for all of the days you spend staring at the path and not knowing what could be ahead, what nobody tells you is that *it's worth it.*

Every last bit.

It's worth it to exchange an illusion of security for the reality of living the way you want, regaining at least some pieces of your life, at least just going for it, at least just trying.

Trying is more than what most people are willing to do anyway.

Nobody knows what's next.

What nobody tells you is that making money from what you love isn't selling out, it's letting your soul support you and fuel you, it's accepting that we all need income to live and if we can do it through our passion, that's great.

What nobody tells you is that though it might be outside the norm, you're not completely an outlier. More people than you can imagine are pursuing similar paths. You're not alone. You never have been. You're not a unicorn. Instead of letting your ego get hurt by this, embrace it. Connect with others going the same way.

What nobody tells you is that the hardest part will be figuring out how to structure your days now that it's all up to you.

This requires discipline.

It requires vision.

It requires commitment.

It requires a lot of self-imposed structure.

It is hard, at first. Then it becomes more freeing over time.

What nobody tells you is that *this is not the easy way out.* This is not necessarily how you opt into a life without any struggle. It's just doing something that makes the struggle worth it.

READ THIS *if* YOU'RE *on the* BRINK *of a* BREAKTHROUGH, *but are* AFRAID *to* TAKE THE LEAP

There is a path to everything you know is waiting for you, even if you don't know what that is right now.

Sometimes, the paths we plan too intently end up limiting us in some way. There are possibilities available to your future self that your current self wouldn't be able to consider. All your mind can pull from is what it's known, and if you're trying to build a life outside of that, then you're going to have to open yourself to the possibility that not only is there a path toward, but that it may very well lead somewhere better than you thought it would.

Sometimes, we don't know because we can't know. The very fact of us knowing would disrupt the timing of what is unfolding. The very fact of us knowing would prevent us from learning the lessons that are here for us today.

And those lessons? They aren't a due we have to pay or a purgatory we are being stuck in, they are the building blocks of the character of the person who is opening up to this next level of their existence. What's here for you right now contains within it the wisdom and the growth needed to unlock the next phase.

I hope that instead of wondering and worrying how you will ever move forward, you can simply recall all the other times you feared you never would...and did. You can remember that you never would have imagined exactly what led you to most good things in your life, and I hope that will inspire you to keep your heart open to wonder, to mystery, to the infinite unknown through which everything beautiful and important will emerge.

I hope you will break loudly, fail toward what matters, let yourself know deep love even if it means you could lose it.

There is no merit in holding back, nothing gained but a life half lived. If you can say nothing else of yourself, say that you had courage. Say that at least you tried. And even if you never quite arrive, allow your legacy to be one of tenacity, one where you did not allow the fear to stop you from doing what you were born to do or having the life you were meant to experience.

If you screw it up, you screw it up. If you get your heart smashed into a million pieces, you get your heart smashed. If you say the wrong thing, you say the wrong thing.

Please do not allow one more moment of your brief and beautiful life to pass where you remain paralyzed beneath the fear of not doing everything just perfectly—a fear that has led you to resist doing anything meaningful at all.

The truth is that the very people who fear such things so deeply are often the same ones who have the most to offer, who have the most honest hearts and willing minds.

We did not come here to arrive at death untouched and unmoved, precisely as we were at the beginning.

The world needs more people like you to show up bravely.

Even if you never get to the other side, will you be alright if you go your entire life knowing you never even tried?

Maybe the kindest possible thing you could do for yourself right now is just be honest with yourself.

Trust yourself.

Know that your feelings are valid and maybe they're trying to move you somewhere you've never been before.

Maybe the kindest possible thing you could do for yourself is to be your whole self, even if you fear you won't be accepted. Maybe the kindest thing you could do is to be as open to your own soul as you can be, even if not everyone understands you.

Maybe the kindest possible thing you could do for yourself is to stop smoothing out every feeling that moves you from the comfortable path—knowing that maybe this urge comes from somewhere and maybe it has a greater purpose.

Maybe you will give someone else permission to be their honest selves. Maybe you will be their living proof that more is possible. Maybe you will become the kind of guide for others that you yourself never had.

And maybe in the end, the kindest possible thing you could do for yourself is to know that there is nothing that holds us back more than the important words that went unspoken, the deep instincts that went unfelt, the callings that went unanswered.

Your life is reaching toward you, and maybe the kindest possible thing you could do is reach back.

As time goes on, you will begin to see the magic in the process. You will begin to understand why things had to happen precisely the way they did. You will realize that if you did not have the exact experiences you had just as you had them, you would have missed out on some essential lessons and tools and pieces of wisdom that built you into the person you are today—the person who will keep walking you forward.

When you look back on the past, you can see the purpose in how everything unfolded, and I am here to tell you that one day, you'll see it in what's happening right now, too. You just have to keep going. One day, you are going to look back on this time and realize you were always right where you were meant to be.

16 WAYS EMOTIONALLY INTELLIGENT PEOPLE *interpret* NEGATIVE FEELINGS *differently*

At the heart of discomfort is the potential for great wisdom. Every time we find ourselves feeling jealous, angry, regretful, resentful, self-hating, judgmental, closed-minded, and hopeless, we are also being handed an opportunity to transform our mindsets and change our lives.

These emotions are not punishments, they're signals of the shifts that need to take place to support the lives we deeply desire to create. Here are 16 of the most important ones.

"What I envy in others is showing me what I desire for myself."

Envy is a revealing emotion. It masks itself as anger or frustration when in reality it is a deeply buried desire.

What we envy in others is actually a cue for us to become clearer about what we want to create for ourselves. We aren't actually trying to say *they don't deserve that*, but rather, *I want to feel like I deserve that, too.* Jealousy reveals our own self-suppression.

When you see someone else actively (or seemingly effortlessly) giving themselves permission to pursue something, your response is to project your own feelings of inadequacy on them. *If you can't do it, why should they?*

Instead of letting envy turn you into the pettiest version of yourself, you can understand that within the thing you envy is a truth about what you should be working toward, not what you should be criticizing someone else for having.

"My feelings are messengers, but I don't have to act on every one of them."

The funny thing about feelings is that in our quest to validate them (which is the only way to release them) it can often seem like we are making them more real.

Not everything we feel is reflective of reality or the way things actually are. You've probably had the experience of thinking someone was "the one" when they weren't, or that you weren't good enough when you certainly were, and so on and so forth.

Instead of responding to our emotions impulsively, we can observe them and then question them. *Is this helpful? Is this truthful? Is this coming from a place of clear perspective, or a lingering past wound?*

Trace it back to its origin, and then extract the lesson that's waiting for you. You'll know you've done this successfully when you emerge with a new inner narrative that's wiser, more accurate, and that makes you feel at ease.

"What I wish I had done yesterday is showing me what I need to do today."

I'll let you in on a dirty little secret: there are thousands of things you regret in your past that you don't have conscious knowledge of. The reason why they remain in the recesses of your mind is that they are ultimately unhelpful to your present or your future.

The things that you actively and persistently regret are actually signaling you not toward what you wish you had done in the past, but toward what you want and need to create going forward.

Instead of thinking back on all you wish you did, devise another way to have that experience now, or in the years to come. There's never just one opportunity to do something important in life.

There's just one opportunity to do it *in that specific way,* but ultimately, there are probably dozens of roads toward your destination, you just have to choose not to stop the journey just because one was a dead end.

"I probably see myself more negatively than anybody else."

Not even your worst critics are judging you as much as you are judging yourself. They're still watching a highlight reel while you're reviewing all of the behind-the-scenes footage.

Nobody else has access to all of the knowledge that you have about yourself, so there's no possible way they could perceive you as negatively as you see yourself. Beyond that, most people think of others positively, or at least neutrally, until they're given a reason not to. This means that most people either think of you pretty well, in an indifferent manner, or not at all.

All of those intense and relentless self-criticisms are just that—*self*-criticism. Nobody is sitting around thinking about that embarrassing thing you did 5 years ago, or evaluating how much progress you are or aren't making in life. They're sitting around and thinking about themselves.

"Other people most likely think I'm doing better than I think I am."

In a similar way, other people are far more likely to value your accomplishments and attributes whereas you focus more on your shortcomings and failures.

This should help you realize that you don't have anything to prove to anyone else, *success is a self-evident thing.*

When you approach other people imagining that they at least have a relatively positive view of you, it changes the way you act around them. Instead of acting on the defense, you can connect, knowing that they probably already think you're worthy (because you are).

"If I just accomplish one thing today, that is enough."

You don't desire to be constantly productive because the world is telling you to be, you desire to be constantly productive because you're afraid of lack. You're afraid of failing, you're afraid of instability, you're afraid of falling behind.

While the world has certainly instilled a culture (and social structure) that makes these fears more common, it's important that we redirect the blame here, and put the onus back on ourselves.

If we never confront our scary feelings of self-doubt, we're going to push ourselves to overwork (and overcompensate) until we die.

We can change the narrative by approaching productivity in a more realistic way. Some days, you'll get it all done. Some days, you need to rest. Some days, just getting one thing checked off the list is reason enough to feel proud of yourself.

Instead of trying to feel less guilt as a rebellion against a world that you think is out to get you, see it as a recalibrating of your mindset to something more rational. Small steps, taken almost daily, move you closer toward stability and success.

You don't need to do it *all* in order to be safe.

"I am allowed to express and process deep emotions."

Some days, life will knock you off your feet. The problem is that instead of embracing heavy waves of emotion, we resist them, and end up with an intense backup that makes us constantly tense and constantly on edge.

The way we remedy this is by shifting the way we approach our feelings in the present moment. Doing this does not mean you are falling behind. It does not mean you are a lesser being. It does not mean you are backtracking. It does not mean you are self-sabotaging. If just means you're processing—and that's a good thing.

When we don't allow ourselves to have these very vulnerable, very human moments, it turns us into hypersensitive robots constantly trying to control our lives and the lives of those around us out of the fear that any trigger might unleash the avalanche.

We can better assimilate ourselves to emotional health by allowing ourselves to lay down, cry it out, vent, and embrace the low tides when they come, knowing the dawn will always rise.

"I am entitled to my own idea of myself."

You are allowed to invent an image of yourself separate from the pieces you put together of what other people have *told you* about yourself. That's how you create your self-esteem as a child, but as an adult, you have to grow out of it.

Instead of just accepting that you're the sum of how others see you, you are free to create a self-perception that is more accurate to your honest experience of yourself. A truly healthy self-image includes good and bad (as all people have) and is built outside of how you *imagine* other people see you.

"I can define what success will look like in my own life."

You build your concept of success by picking up on micro-cues from the people around you, and what you've heard them say is and isn't acceptable in life. You build your idea of success around the ultimate vision of what would make you most loved.

That is until you realize it's a fruitless endeavor. Eventually, you reach the peak of that particular mountain only to find that you've fulfilled someone else's vision while you yourself feel empty inside. It's no place to be, and yet, somewhere we all must usually arrive before we know how to redirect.

You are allowed to define success on your own terms. You are allowed to say what is or isn't enough for your life.

One way that you can help yourself do this more easily is to stop deciding what success is or isn't for someone else and wish them well on their own journey, knowing a great life looks different for us all.

"My purpose might not be my job, and it doesn't have to be."

Your job pays the bills. Your purpose gives meaning to your life. No one person has any single purpose. Our purpose can change day-to-day, hour-to-hour. Our purpose may be found in a relationship or our presence, or a job we do for a while, and then another one we do later on.

Our purpose is *just to be alive.*

Everything else that follows is likewise important, but if you get too caught up in the idea that you have to find your divine purpose within a profession, you seriously limit yourself and your understanding of true and pervasive meaning. You also attach your worth to something temporary, when your purpose is an infinite expression of your own nature.

Instead of trying to figure out what you're supposed to do *for the rest of your existence,* figure out what the next right step is in your life—because that's probably the way forward.

"Nobody is required to live up to my expectations of them."

Resentment is often bred from unfulfilled (and unfair) expectations. Absolutely nobody is required to live up to our ideas of who we think they should or shouldn't be or what they should or shouldn't do, in the same way that we are not required to live up to those ideas they have about us.

This is where boundaries come in. While we cannot control who or what someone becomes, we can control our interactions with them, and we must. Because when we assume that everyone is required to be who we think they should be, we place limitations on them, and we ultimately just make ourselves frustrated and resentful.

We can either embrace people for who they are in this moment or decide to limit the presence they have in our lives.

"It is safe to let go of the past experiences once I've extracted the lesson from them."

You don't have to keep ruminating. You don't have to keep reviewing the details of old experiences. You don't have to keep worrying that you'll get caught off guard again.

When we can't let go of the past, it's often because it doesn't feel safe to. Without hypervigilance, we assume the threat will be free to come up and surprise us again.

The experiences we can't release often still hold within them a lesson that has yet to be extracted. Once we've learned from the mistake and carry that wisdom with us each day, we are free to finally release what brought it to us. When we haven't learned the lesson, it doesn't feel safe to release the teacher.

"Right now, my mission is to make the very best of what is in front of me."

Instead of constantly thinking about where you should or shouldn't be, or who does or doesn't have more or less than you, or how you measure up to your friends or family or past selves, you can instead think of the only task any one of us truly have, which is simply *to make the best of what's in front of us.* That's it.

Make the best of this day. Make the best of the opportunities you have. Make the best of your current relationships. Make the best of yourself—right here, and right now.

"The best" doesn't mean "the most perfect." It just means that instead of passively letting life happen to you, you show up in each moment and you work with what you have, instead of just complaining about what you don't.

"My most persistent judgments of other people are often a reflection of a block within myself."

What you dislike about other people can reveal a lot about your own psyche.

Most importantly though, your ongoing relational issues are often pointing toward emotional blocks within yourself, the very blocks that are holding you back from the life you're asking for—which is why they're in your conscious awareness.

If you don't acknowledge someone else's progress, you can't acknowledge your own. If you villainize someone else's success, you resist your own. If you sum someone up by their worst traits, you sum yourself up by your own.

And what you will almost always come to find is that the moments at which you feel most compelled to judge and shrink other people from your life is the very moment at which you yourself feel pretty small.

Instead of projecting, seek deeper wisdom. Heal your relationship with yourself, and the rest will fall into place.

"I do not need to feel guilty over what I cannot control."

There's no sense in holding onto what you can no longer change. You don't have to feel guilty for the sake of it. Guilting yourself doesn't make you a better person, it makes you a *bitter* person, which inevitably results in less-than-admirable behavior.

Instead of trying to bully yourself into better character, seek a deeper understanding of why you acted the way you did, and what blind spots led you there.

Understanding the root of the behavior more completely will not only ensure that you change your actions going forward, but it will give you a greater sense of peace because you're trusting in your wisdom, not your impulses.

"I am more powerful than I think I am."

When you realize that your words, your actions, and your beliefs deeply impact not only your reality but the realities of those around you, you start taking yourself a lot more seriously.

You start to realize that you do have the power to change your life, to create what you desire, to experience another reality.

Instead of trying to move the unmovable or change the unchangeable, you recognize that you can control a number of things that are right in front of you, and then over time, you will be able to shift more and more.

"My highest potential future life already exists."

When you close your eyes and imagine your future self or your future life, the one that feels so good, so right, so inspiring, and so hopeful—what you need to know is that *it already exists.*

That person is you. That life is yours.

The journey is bridging the gap between visualizing it and seeing it in reality. That journey contains releasing attachments, changing behaviors, shifting your belief system, and slowly taking action every day until you reach the other side.

You are destined for what you most desire.

The truths that pull you deeply do so for a reason.

You are inching closer toward the life that was always meant to be yours, but the first step in enacting it completely is knowing that *it's already there*.

It's yours for the taking.

WHEN *you're* READY *to* TAKE *your* POWER BACK, BEGIN HERE

No matter how much inner work you've done, no matter how resilient you've become, no matter how future-proofed you once believed your plans to be—life sometimes hands you the occasional reminder that you are not entirely a god unto yourself.

You coexist with billions of other creators.

Our worlds merge and collide, and sometimes, they collapse.

When you lose your inner power, it's not really gone. It's just buried under the belief that there is something beyond you that has the capacity to limit what your life will become. It's been hollowed out from thinking that whatever disrupted you will block your path forever.

When you lose your power, it's because something came along and removed your sense of certainty.

Some event made you realize that you can't always predict what's next. It forced you to reconcile the fact that you are still just human. You began to suspect that there are elements within our lives that we cannot always anticipate, nor make sense of once they've arrived.

If you've lost your power, it's because you're resisting this truth.

In place of acceptance, you've put hyper-vigilance.

You've spent your days mulling over the details, tracing and dissecting the events and how they started and ended, back to front and front to back, again and again. You've observed and you've found patterns. You've psychoanalyzed. You've become wholly consumed by the offhand chance that this disruption might arise again, and in that consumption, you've lost your will to press forward.

What you don't realize is that your obsession is acting as a shield, albeit not a strong one.

You are assuming that you can only be safe if you allow the intrusive thoughts to make a home in your head. If you let them circulate until they embed themselves in your subconscious, encode into your identity, play out through your daily actions, then maybe—just maybe— you can do what you didn't before,which is avoid them entirely.

Of course, what you aren't seeing is that by giving your power over to something that is beyond you, you are making it even stronger. What holds our mental power is where we place our thoughts, and then our beliefs, and then our trust, and then our faith.

We cannot always trust the world.

Therefore, we must find the resolve to trust ourselves.

To trust yourself is not to believe that you will never again be hurt.

To trust yourself is not to think that you're safer for playing small.

To trust yourself means that you will dare to step forward, despite all odds, no matter what's up against you, no matter what forces may be at work. To trust yourself means that you are no longer content to lodge your soul in the circumstances that have long stopped serving you. To trust yourself means that you will no longer accept fear reprogramming you, reorienting your values and changing your perspective to one that is simply holding you back.

Healing is the ultimate vulnerability.

It does not mean we arrive on the other side magically declaring that we're the victor, but that we show up humbly, with our hearts wounded but open.

Healing is to accept hurting as part of being human.

Healing is to carry on anyway.

When you are ready to take your power back, it probably won't come from an inspired place of sound resolve.

It will come from sheer desperation, a final battle cry. It will arise from your last ditch effort to save your own life.

You will know that it's time to take your power back when there is no other viable choice, because in the aftermath of loss, you discovered that you unraveled your own existence so that nothing could be taken from you again.

You can't lose your power.

It's not something separate from you.

It's never lost, just buried beneath the desire to keep your true self safe.

And that part of you—the one that really wants to protect you? Maybe that's your power speaking in a different way. Maybe that's not a sign that you've abandoned yourself, but that you love yourself enough to safeguard whatever small parts of your heart remain untouched.

Maybe the path forward is to find gratitude for the fact that we wanted to shield ourselves in the first place. Maybe recognizing your power is seeing it take on an entirely new form, one that we honor for its presence, and then release in place of something more helpful.

> *The path forward is understanding that we are sometimes collateral damage to people's own inner wars, and that we do not need to adopt their weapons as our own in order to fight back.*

> *The path forward is realizing that our sanctuary is within ourselves, and our power is impenetrable. It is there, resting, and waiting, until we are ready to act on it again.*

When that day comes, the day we are ready to begin again, we almost always find that doing so is less a feat of willpower, and more the willingness to let our souls back into our days again.

It often begins with allowing yourself to enjoy something small, because you deserve that. It grows when you allow yourself to care for yourself, because you deserve that, too. It swells when you allow yourself to acknowledge how far you've come, and for every piece of yourself you can't stand, there are a thousand others that are so much more beautiful, so much more worthy, so much more admired and cared for.

You deserve that, too.

> *Your power is not being able to exert your will on everyone around you.*

It's also not watering down your life until you're the most acceptable possible version of yourself.

It's having the courage to hurt, and then heal.

It's being willing to try again.

It's not that nothing bad can ever happen, but that we won't reject all of the goodness that still exists even if it does.

13 THINGS YOU NEED *to* STOP DOING *if you* TRULY WANT *to* MOVE YOUR LIFE FORWARD

If you're ready to move your life forward, begin by getting still.

Often, feeling stuck isn't about not having enough momentum or willpower, but about being in misalignment with your needs, wants and strategies.

It's not that you're not trying hard enough, but that you're *too attached to things that aren't right for you.*

If you want to be in a completely different place by this time next year, you're going to have to get honest with yourself. You're going to have to stop using busy-ness as a distraction, you're going to have to replace quantity with quality, you're going to have to do some soul-searching, and you're going to have to learn to prioritize what your future self will thank you for.

Here are the 13 most potent shifts you can make to get your life back on track.

01 | Stop waiting for perfect circumstances.

I know that it feels like your life is on an indefinite pause.

If you wait for perfect circumstances to take the leap, start the business, build up what you already have, make a life change, move, course-correct, go on an inner journey, travel, start investing, find peace, be grateful, enjoy what you have or begin your new adventure—you will be waiting forever.

Perfect circumstances *do not* exist.

There are certainly cases where some times may be more advantageous than others, and timing itself is important, but it's also out of your control.

You can't exist in a perma-state of waiting for something outside of you to shift before you feel like you have the green light to shift something within.

> *You have to start now. You have to adapt here. You have to do what you can with what you have.*

Even if some circumstances are less ideal than others, if you're subconsciously looking for a reason to play it safe, you'll always find one. You're never going to wake up one day and feel completely ready, completely fearless, completely assured.

You arrive there by beginning, and then continuing, despite every reason why you shouldn't, or thought you couldn't, or previously wouldn't.

You have to stop waiting for perfect circumstances.

You have to create them instead.

02 | Stop confusing your maximum output with your maximum potential.

Your maximum potential isn't doing the most work humanly possible each day. It's not about trying to capitalize on every single moment of every single hour, thinking you can bullet-journal and morning routine into a robotic state of perfect functioning.

You are a human being.

> *Your maximum potential is creating a life that is peaceful and meaningful to you. It is doing less, but better.*

Making the "most of every moment" doesn't mean trying to force yourself to over-perform and overcorrect until you're a washed out version of the person you could have been.

Getting to your maximum potential means creating a daily routine that makes you feel *most like yourself,* where your activities, commitments and decisions reflect your values, and what your future self would thank you for doing.

03 | Stop spending your peak hours on things you don't care about.

We all have to pay the bills and cook dinner and wipe the countertops.

There are always going to be less than desirable tasks that are essential to the function of being human and staying alive.

The point isn't that you get to a place where you can avoid those tasks altogether, but that you get to a place where they're no longer occupying your peak hours.

Your peak hours are the time each day when you're clearest, most energized, most capable of problem-solving, getting inspired, and creating. For most people, this is early morning to mid-morning.

Don't waste your most potent energy on things that drain you.

Use it to build what will matter most for your future.

Instead of waking up to check social media and the news or rush around your house to get ready and start work on time, try to amend your routine so that you wake up earlier and get to enjoy your coffee, find time to meditate or journal, work on writing, business building, or even spending time with someone you love.

> *The way you use your energy each day plants the seeds of the harvest you'll reap in the future.*

Spend them wisely.

04 | Stop only seeing your life through other people's eyes.

We are hardwired to feel as though being acceptable to others is survival and safety. Trying to completely "not care what other people think" is impossible. It's not a matter of you not being mentally strong enough, it's just not how any of us were designed to think.

So instead of trying to convince yourself not to care about anyone else's opinion (because honestly, you *should* care about what *some* people think) try instead to refrain from seeing your life only through other people's eyes.

Most people don't see or interpret life for themselves, they do it based on the way they imagine other people would perceive it, namely, a small handful of people whose acceptance or approval feels most vital to secure.

Instead of trying to project and imagine their opinions, learn to consider them, and then also consider your own.

How do *you* feel about this?

If nobody else was around, or would ever know anything about your life ever again, how would *you* live?

It's about existing in a way that's in authentic alignment to who you are, not what's in forced alignment to who someone else is.

05 | Stop believing that timing is everything.

Timing is something you surrender to, not something you allow to control you.

If you don't just start now, you risk spending the better part of the coming years in a state of limbo. It's never the "right time" to do anything big, important, and scary. We will always have reasons to delay. We will always feel uncomfortable when facing the unknown. We will always have counter arguments and alternative plans.

Eventually you have to decide what matters to you, and then you have to commit to staying the course, no matter how the tides may turn.

> *There is no perfect timing, there is just time, and what we do with how much we are given.*

Instead of waiting for the perfect moment to arise, consider instead that the time you have each day is like having a set amount of money in a bank account that expires at the end of each day.

What you don't use, you lose.

06 | Stop changing course so often.

You can't keep changing your plans, your strategy, or your goals, and expect to get anywhere significant.

You're not going to feel any kind of radical shift by committing to a new practice for only a few days.

You're not going to see any real results if you don't stick with a business strategy for at least a year or two, minimum.

> *Sometimes, we change course to get back on track. More often, we amend our approach because we're afraid to really begin.*

Be honest with yourself about which category you fall into.

Do you really need to keep making so many shifts, or are you resisting the work that truly needs to be done, which is settling into what you have, rooting into where you are, embracing the person you've always been, and simply allowing yourself to bloom?

07 | Stop thinking you're so out of the ordinary.

Everyone is special in the sense that everyone has a unique set of gifts and talents and perspectives and ways in which they express love and presence that can never be recreated by another human being on the planet.

But we're all still human.

When you have it in your head that you're going at this alone, that you're the only person in the world who's ever navigated a marriage, raised a challenging child, started a new business, managed uncertain finances, or lived through a world crisis, you're not helping yourself out.

Thinking that you're so out of the ordinary is holding you back, because it makes you believe that what you're doing is unpopular, and therefore, unsafe or wrong.

Sure, your choices or circumstances may be markedly different from the "norm," but what is the "norm" really, other than the mix of environment, peer group, family, religion, government, and media you were exposed to throughout your life?

Whatever you're doing, there are probably millions of other people who have also tried it, done it, or are also doing it.

You're special, but *you're not alone.*

08 | Stop thinking short-term.

Instant gratification is alluring, but not helpful.

You need to be thinking in long-term strides.

Not just how to get through tomorrow, but what the next best step in your career would be to arrive where you'd like to be by retirement. Not what get-rich-quick stock you could magically uncover and strike gold with, but how to consistently invest in a diversified portfolio and allow it to grow with time, even if you start small.

It's not just what would feel good now, but also what you'll thank yourself for later.

While there's always a time to treat yourself and enjoy life, it has to be balanced by principles, values, and forward thinking.

Otherwise, you'll keep treading water and wondering why you're still not approaching the shore.

09 | Stop assuming you always know best.

This doesn't instill confidence in the way you think it might.

More often, it makes you feel hopeless and defeated, because when challenges arise, you think that you know the only solution, the only answer, and the only viable outcome for your life.

Let life surprise you.

Let experts help you.

Let people who are wiser than you show you the way forward.

Instead of thinking you know the only way forward, consider that maybe you don't know exactly what you need in a partner, and be open to different types of people. Consider the idea that you don't know exactly what work is right for you, and be open to experimenting. Allow yourself to sit with the idea that there are incredible things right within your reach that you do not realize, because you were never taught.

You do not have all the answers, even if you have many of them.

Nobody does.

Life is an unfolding.

Let things in that you didn't previously choose.

You will be better for it.

10 | Stop underestimating the power of inner work.

The truth about forward movement is that it's more about present stillness than anything else.

> *Can you sit with yourself?*

> *Can you be present?*

> *Can you allow yourself to metabolize the feelings that keep coming up?*

> *Can you ask yourself the tough questions to get the important answers?*

> *Are you willing to change your mind?*

> *Are you willing to change your life?*

While there are many parts of life that are out of your control, the parts that are within it are often a reflection of you.

When you commit to working on yourself, that effort radiates out and touches everything and everyone around you. So commit to growth. Commit to becoming better. Decide that you're ready to expand your heart past its current perimeters.

There is so much more waiting for you, but you have to be open to it first.

11 | Stop playing down your dreams.

If fortune favors the brave, then it also prefers the bold.

Not only do you need to have a strong vision about what you want to create next in your life, you also need to be ambitious. You need to think beyond the limits of your current perspective. You need to be daring.

This isn't just because aiming higher inevitably raises your expectations overall, but also because *boldness often tells you what you're actually capable of, though you might not yet believe it.*

If you're willing to believe that something *might* be possible for you—it already is.

The virtue of you even being willing to consider it means that it's somewhere within your realm of possibility already. It's just a matter of first realizing it, and then acting on it.

12 | Stop avoiding your discomfort.

Discomfort signals that a shift needs to be made.

Discomfort, much like anger, grief, and jealousy, is a healthy human emotion that communicates something to us. It's not the feeling itself that's unhealthy, but that we do not know what to do with it when it arises.

Anger is the healthy response to injustice, or a boundary being crossed. Grief is the healthy response to loss. Jealousy is the healthy response to seeing someone else pursue what you are resisting. Likewise, discomfort is the healthy response to knowing it's time to make a change. Discomfort is not trying to punish you, it's trying to help you.

However, most people can't simply sit with it long enough to let it tell them what it needs to say, let alone take the next step, which is often to temporarily endure *more* discomfort before a solution is found.

Discomfort is an experience most people are not willing to face or feel.

This is why their lives stay as they are.

13 | Stop thinking that the worst possible outcome is you making a wrong choice.

The reason why so many people resist making change, despite wanting and needing it, is that they believe that they could "misstep" in life. The idea is that what they have is good or good enough, and by taking a leap, there's a chance they could fall entirely off path, and ruin something that was alright while trying to pursue something better.

This is faulty logic.

> *There are very few choices in life that we can't amend or at least adjust as we go on. The world does not punish us for choosing one thing over another, we punish ourselves out of fear and desire to conform to the most simple, unchallenging path.*

I know that it seems like the worst possible outcome is the idea of you potentially making a wrong choice, but the worst possible outcome is you never living your life, never experiencing the depth and beauty of existence, never pursuing your dreams, never becoming fulfilled, never finding meaning…all because you were too afraid to maybe get it wrong.

A misstep isn't the worst thing that can happen.

Refusing to move forward is.

WITHIN *the* EMOTIONS YOU *are* AFRAID *to* FEEL EXISTS *the* WISDOM YOUR SOUL *is* WAITING *to* RECEIVE

On the surface, our emotions always seem to be compelling us to react.

We assume that as soon as we feel something deeply, we should respond to it immediately, and that the deeper it is, the more real it is. It's like we are still operating from our most base instincts, as though some abstract fear of not-enoughness translates to the imminent survival of our very beings.

This impulse can often lead us to resist those emotions, fearing not that they would last forever, but that if we allowed ourselves to experience them completely, they would drive us to make choices that we'd have to live with forever.

In some ways, this is a form of wisdom. At least on some level, we are acknowledging that our feelings should be evaluated before they're responded to, lest we make a choice we'll regret later on.

But what if this is also the very reason we feel so stuck?

What if, within the very emotions you're resisting, exists some code of wisdom your subconscious mind needs in order to sort your reality and make your next move? What if you trying to write a story about what the feeling means and what you should do about it is you avoiding feeling it in the first place? What if it is only through the fullest processing of those emotions that your body will be able to absorb the critical information needed at a subconscious level to better inform your experience?

What if, instead of overthinking, instead of overanalyzing, instead of trying to figure out what you need to do next, you sat down and allowed yourself to feel what you feel in the moment you want to feel it? What if you decided that, just for a moment, you wouldn't react or make decisions while you were in this state, but rather, you would just be there?

What if you could accept that living a purposeful or meaningful or aligned life does not mean you can avoid these feelings altogether, because they are not punishments, they are guides? What if you could instead learn to trust the wisdom your bodies possess, allowing it to receive genuine feedback so it can make the shifts necessary to bring you back to your own path?

What if the very reason why you keep spinning yourself in circles is because you are taking action before the emotion is completely processed, and so you're missing a piece of the information you need?

What if there's nothing wrong with you, but rather, something that needs to be adjusted within your life, something that you have not let yourself feel, let alone address?

What if before you can gain clarity, you simply need rest?

What if your life gets stuck and stagnates when you stop allowing yourself to feel, and so your emotional navigation system goes on pause? What if your mind's attempts to interrupt the full release of those emotions is actually what's keeping them stuck? What if you don't need to demand answers right now, but allow yourself to process the fullest extent of your experiences until you feel reset again?

What if you allowed yourself a safe space to emotionally process, and then allowed yourself to rise the next morning in the calm, and trusted that you would know what to do?

What if instead of trying to put this all on a timeline, and with a decided end-goal, and with a list of questions that needed to be answered, you surrendered it all up to the greatest wisdom you could muster within you, a wisdom that can only be gained by allowing your soul to bear witness to what you do not want to feel?

The next time you realize your heart is still white-hot with anger and grief, I hope you will simply allow yourself to feel that without pressuring yourself to be more at peace.

The next time you think "I should be okay," I hope you will not shame yourself into silencing the very instinct within you that is shouting, you are meant for more than this.

When I say you are meant for more, I mean that you're meant for relationships that fulfill and energize you. I mean that you're meant to be appreciated and seen. I mean that you're mean to know yourself at your core. I mean that you're meant to experience something within this life, and only you will know what that is. Whether it's hard or easy, simple or complex, happening tomorrow or in ten years, you will know it when it arrives, because it will leave you in a state of wonder, and grace.

A life of more is not one that always expands outward, it's very often one that opens up inward.

I hope you will consider that maybe that's possible for you.

I hope you will slowly learn that you can live without a problem to solve or mountain to climb. I hope you will realize that your existence will not always be a constant well of longing, because once our thirst is quenched, we do not want for more.

I hope you will slowly learn how to invest your energy not into resisting what you feel, but building what will be out of the wisdom your experiences have given you. I hope you will realize that your first choice doesn't have to be your last one, no number of wrong steps will ever make your path disappear completely. I hope you will realize that the world is bendable, and your life is changeable. You did not arrive here to grit through the experiences other people have chosen for you, but to eventually decide upon your own.

I hope you will know that you can live within the questions.

You can feel what you feel without letting it compel you to burn everything down.

You can witness, simply observe.

You can allow your body to absorb knowledge at a level far deeper than you yourself could reach.

And when the instructions that wisdom offers surface at the top of your mind, I hope you will be ready to walk.

Your life is waiting on the other side.

10 SIGNS YOU'RE ACTUALLY MAKING PROGRESS *in* LIFE, EVEN *if it doesn't* FEEL LIKE YOU ARE

Even here, even now—you are growing.

I know it seems like the only way to measure your progress is by timing, milestones, and goals reached, but in reality, progress is more about how we get into alignment with what we need and want, and less about how perfectly we paint the outward picture of what we think we're supposed to be.

This is why it is often the most counterintuitive times that provide us the most opportunity for growth.

Here are a few signs that you're actually making incredible progress in life, even if it doesn't feel like you are.

01 | You've lost relationships.

Maybe you look back and feel sad about everyone you've lost touch with.

Maybe you reflect on all of your would-be relationships, and whether or not you tried hard enough. Maybe you think of all the friends and acquaintances that have crossed your path and regret not remaining closer. Maybe you look back at all the support you had, and wonder why you ever chose to move onto your own path.

Losing relationships is often a sign that we're growing into the people we are supposed to be.

We aren't meant to have the exact same circle of friends and acquaintances for the entirety of our lives. Unless those people grow in perfect congruence with us, we often step out of pace with them as they head down their own paths in life. This isn't necessarily a bad thing. It's not a sign of failure.

In fact, the willingness to let go of social comfort in order to pursue what feels more authentic to you is a sign of massive, incredible growth.

We don't lose relationships because we're not worthy of them, we lose them because we're mismatched to them. That's usually a good indicator that we've grown, we've changed, and we need to realign with people who understand who we're becoming, not just who we've been.

02 | You're doubting your next step.

If you're not doubting your next step, it's not the right step.

I know that seems wrong, as though the most correct thing would absolve any doubt, any fear or any worry from your mind. The more right it is, the more you're going to have an unconscious, emotional, and often embodied reaction.

You're scared because you care. You're doubting because this actually means something to you. You're nervous because it's unfamiliar.

You're finally choosing something you actually desire, you're confronting the limiting beliefs that have held you back from it all this time, and you're actually putting something on the line for once.

You're no longer content to follow someone else's success script. You're no longer just passively floating through your existence. You're making a choice, and that comes with discomfort, that comes with responsibility, and often, that comes with fear.

Too many people won't leap because they're afraid of that initial jolt, but they also never learn to spread their wings, and they never arrive anywhere else.

03 | You feel slightly embarrassed of your past self.

When you think back to who you were even just a year ago, you might cringe.

While this is an incredibly valid experience to have—and a common one at that—please know that it's not a sign that you were an awful person before, but that you're coming into greater self-awareness about who you do and do not want to be.

Please know that nobody is, or ever was, judging you as much as you are judging yourself right now.

In addition, this is a natural part of the process of positive disintegration. Your old self is no longer suited to manage the life you have today, and so they must transform into who you are becoming now.

04 | You're slowing down.

Rather than rapid, intense acceleration, you're interested in mindful, intentional decision making.

When we slow down, it's because we're no longer just running away from what's wrong, but learning to step toward what's right.

Maybe you realized that you needed a break.

Maybe you saw clearly that your workload was unsustainable.

Maybe you finally came to terms with the fact that you've been overextended and burnt out, and something had to give eventually.

Instead of trying to push through all of your body's signals that you're doing too much, growth is when we slow down and start to listen to what they've been trying to say all along.

In this stillness and rest, we often find answers we didn't know we were asking for.

05 | You're starting to care more about how you feel as opposed to what other people think.

You're no longer content to live a life designed to appease everyone but yourself.

Sometimes, this can emerge as a sort of anger or aggression. You find yourself completely fed up with everyone's judgements and shortcomings, and you might feel like you want to lash out or cut ties with those people so that you can relieve yourself from some of the pressure.

There are boundaries to be set here, and first and foremost, that begins with you.

You have to start by making decisions for *your life*, not your parent's lives, not your friend's lives, not your partner's life, not your peers' lives.

When you start stepping forward in your full truth, give people a chance to respond to you instead of just assuming how they'll react.

You can make a call about your relationship from there.

If, on the other hand, you're looking back on instances in which you didn't set boundaries that you should have and are regretting your lack of self-respect, write it all down. Put it in a drawer and come back to it tomorrow. Is there anything there worth sharing with the people involved? Would it bring you peace to approach them and let them know how you feel, or would it just bring more stress?

That's a decision you can make for yourself, but first, just know that it's a great sign of growth that you're actually angry enough to stop living by an invisible set of rules set forth by people who do not have to walk in your shoes.

06 | You're processing feelings you forgot about.

Displaced emotions are feelings that either don't have a discernible root, or seem like an overreaction given the situation.

Often, these feelings are actually related to something entirely different, and have been triggered by your current circumstances.

In the same way that your body sheds skin cells and excess waste each day, this is yet another way that your body releases memories and emotional responses from your tissues and cells.

This will probably be more pronounced if you have a history of suppressing the way you feel.

Either way, give yourself some grace, and some credit.

You are doing a really good job sorting through some really heavy stuff.

07 | **You're aware of what's wrong, even if you don't know what would be right.**

I know that it seems like your life should unfold from a place of revelation; that one day, you'll wake up and have clarity about exactly what you want and when and where.

That's almost never how it works.

Real change is almost always catalyzed not by a feeling of inspiration, but a feeling of discontent.

> *Before you'll know what's right, you'll know what's wrong.*

This is the scariest part because without the answers, it seems like the questions are never-ending. It seems like you're stuck. It seems like there's no way out.

There is, you just haven't thought of it yet.

This makes sense because you've also never come to terms fully with what's really not working in your life.

When you have the courage to do one, you often find the other.

08 | You're experiencing serendipitous alignment.

Even if you still feel completely stuck where you are right now, you're still starting to connect the dots.

Perhaps an opportunity has arisen that you didn't think would. Maybe you happen to meet the right person at the right time; maybe you see or hear something that you can't help but attribute to being a "sign." Maybe something comes together mysteriously well, even despite all of your doubts that it wouldn't.

It doesn't all have to be finished right now.

The fact that a few pieces are coming together is enough.

> *What's meant for you will come to you, and it will stay with you for as long as it needs to.*

In this process, you're starting to learn that part of building a life you really want isn't just controlling the inputs and outcomes, but also surrendering to possibilities so good, you might not have thought to ask for them.

There's often a plan greater than yours, but it's not until we surrender that we truly understand the redirection.

09 | You're more concerned with being happy than being successful.

Whereas you were once mostly interested in earning more, or becoming more, or securing a better-sounding title, you find now that you're trying to build your days around feeling better and enjoying as much as you can.

This is a tremendous sign of progress, though it might look on the surface as though you're doing less and being less ambitious.

> *You're becoming ambitious in the ways that truly matter—your heart, soul, and spirit.*

What if your goal was to enjoy each day as much as you could?

To find one gem of gratitude?

To spend uninterrupted time with your loved ones?

To enjoy the fresh air?

To get a good night's sleep?

What would it take for you to truly feel alive each day?

That's the question you start asking yourself when you are genuinely making unprecedented progress.

10 | You're beginning to understand that there is no "finish line."

If you're like most people, you've probably lived the majority of your life waiting for the "next thing" so that you could finally be happy and free.

Growing up means you realize there is no finish line.

There is no point at which you just coast.

It's a marathon, not a sprint.

Instead of arriving as fast as possible, you're now interested in what would be most sustainable and meaningful long-term.

> *You're never going to feel like you've "made it," and guess what? You don't want to. You don't want the bar to end there. You don't want to peak so soon.*

There is no point after which all of your worries will dissolve and your life will become magically effortless and you'll be happy forevermore.

There is only the ever-present now, and how we show up to it, and how we respond to it.

That's all we can manage.

That's all we can aspire to.

HOW TO REMEMBER YOU'RE NOT ALONE, *even when it* REALLY FEELS *like* YOU ARE

When you feel like you're alone, it's not the aloneness you're afraid of.

You know how to spread your arms across cool sheets at night. You know how to drive with the windows down, letting the cadences of your favorite songs move through you. You know the tranquil peace of slowly setting yourself into a warm bath. You know the strange charm of walking around by yourself, gazing upward and imagining the stories of the city.

You know it is only ever in solitude that we extract the most important truths about our lives. Without the expectations of others around us, we get to see who we most essentially are.

You know what it is to be alone.

It is not aloneness that gives you that pinching and panicked feeling.

It's loneliness—which sounds the same, but is actually different.

Loneliness is what happens when you convince yourself that you're no longer worth connection. Loneliness is what happens when you misbelieve that love is something you get when you're good enough, something you receive when you play by the specific and unrelenting rules of those you're most invested in receiving it from.

That type of connection, though?

It's not connection.

It's hunger.

It's vanity.

It's attachment.

Connection is the free-flowing state of sharing presence with one another, and more people would want to connect with you than you'd probably assume. Connection is recognizing that even when life hands you a season of aloneness, you are never completely disconnected.

You are part of every person you've ever loved.

You are a part of every place you've ever been.

You are cared for even if those who care are no longer present in your day-to-day life.

You almost always have at least one person who will care enough to stay by you, even at your worst.

We all assume that because we live in such a hyperconnected society, we should be less lonely than ever. Not only can we keep in touch with everyone we've ever known, but we can also witness every detail of their lives unfold before us. No human beings prior to this ever experienced society in such a way.

That's exactly the problem.

What we gain in "connection," we lose in context.

People used to move on from old towns and groups and friends, catching up now and again, but generally reserving the intimate details of their lives for those who grew in alignment with them.

This is healthy because it gives us space to find new identities instead of being stuck trying to appease all the different ones we constructed, that have come together all at once, to witness how we are today.

We feel most alone when we are strangers to ourselves, and in a world where everyone is watching, we are more pieces of what they would want us to be than the whole of what we want to become.

We don't know where we fit because our ideas of ourselves are bound up in expectations. We have different faces for different people and somewhere throughout the constant pressure to be something else, we lose something.

Our true selves.

Our real selves.

The selves that know we are permanently and fundamentally connected.

The selves that know we don't need 100 friends to be fulfilled.

We don't even need 10.

Life is not a popularity contest.

It's not about who is best at what and how much so.

It's about that real connection, which is the willingness to show up exactly as we are and realizing we're being met exactly where we are.

· No adjustments.

No shifting.

No hiding.

When we have this type of authentic connection, we end up discovering a sense of unity that we could never piece together from staring at vignettes of someone's life. We begin to understand that those creeping doubts, subtle fears, deep curiosities—they're universal. For how different we are and how much our experiences may vary, there is no human experience you can have that someone else has not had at least a similar version of.

Coming to this realization is simple, but hard.

We have to truly see through the guise of what we thought connection was in an effort to foster it in reality.

We have to truly let go of trying to appeal to every person imaginable in an effort to come home to ourselves.

When life hands us a season of being by ourselves, we have to find the courage to sleep alone and eat alone and dance in the kitchen in our underwear and lay in bed at night and wonder if we are going to be okay.

We do not earn connection.

In the words of Mary Oliver, "You do not have to walk on your knees for a hundred miles through the desert repenting, you only have to let the soft animal of your body love what it loves."

Try to find love for the moments that life has given you to be alone.

Try to find love as you remember that you are already a piece of something far bigger than you, from where you came and where you will return.

Try to find love in the fact that maybe you're being given an opportunity to be introduced to yourself so that you might be able to introduce that person to someone else.

And maybe that was the piece that was missing all along.

7 WAYS *to* BECOME YOUR *most* EMOTIONALLY RESILIENT SELF

Resiliency is not an inherent trait, it is a practice.

In fact, our ability to respond to and cope with life is usually a direct reflection of how many challenges we've been through. It's usually the people who are the most at peace who have also been through the worst that life could offer them.

There's no coincidence in this.

When we learn to respond to our circumstances better, and especially through practice and repetition, we develop the character needed to get through life with more ease.

These are 7 strategies that you can use to not only respond to your emotions, but also learn from them, grow from them, and use them to your advantage.

Lean into how you feel.

Rather than leaning *out* of their emotions, resilient people get clear on what they feel and why.

Instead of leaning away from how they feel (such as one would do through drinking, suppression, or distraction) emotionally resilient people journal, speak with a therapist or trusted friend, or express their experience in some other way that validates it.

Accept it, even if you don't like it.

Accepting something does not mean you're okay with it. It doesn't mean you aren't going to change it. It doesn't mean it's right. Acceptance only means that you are no longer going to stay in denial about reality.

Acceptance is the first step to healing because until we see our circumstances for what they are, changing them becomes impossible. Even if your acceptance looks like you admitting that you're in a crisis and you need help, that's still progress, because you're so much closer to receiving it as opposed to where you would be if you remained in denial.

Speak plainly about your feelings.

When we're all jumbled up in how we feel, the facts about what's really going on can become totally skewed.

A way to instantly calm yourself down and get clear on what's really happening is to speak the facts about the situation, or what you feel about the situation, as simply as you can. This may look like this:

> — *I am on the receiving end of a brutal breakup, one I didn't see coming, and right now I'm feeling lost, unstable, and embarrassed.*

> — *I dislike how I look, and after a lifelong battle to accept myself, I am feeling hopeless that I will ever find peace.*

— I am anxious about my work situation, and though I recognize it is irrational, the feelings are strong and are disrupting my quality of life.

Find your motive.

People who are resilient find the silver lining in anything.

Another way to put this is that they find their motive no matter what's going on. If they are responsible for doing something they don't feel like doing, they imagine what's in it for them. If they are required to go to work, or exercise, or do really anything that isn't immediately satisfying, they focus instead on what benefit they could extract from it.

Instead of thinking that you dislike your one family member so you're dreading the holidays, consider how happy you'll be to see everyone else you love—that should make one individual seem worth dealing with. Instead of thinking that you don't want to go to work, think about your long-term goals, or even just your paycheck. Instead of thinking that you don't want to exercise, think about how much better you'll feel after you do, or how accomplished you'll feel at the end of the week.

In anything life has to offer, there is always a benefit to be found. Emotionally resilient people find it.

Learn to laugh at yourself.

Humor is an incredible tool to diffuse otherwise tense and difficult situations.

If you're able to make a joke about what you're going through, or find something funny and ridiculous within your own behavior, you'll likely find yourself much more able to cope with what's going on. Humor instantly lightens any situation, and when you don't take everything so seriously, it alleviates so much unnecessary pressure.

Solve the problem.

More often than not, there is some kind of action that we can take in order to resolve whatever is bothering us.

In fact, we often find that the things that irritate us most are the ones that are pointing toward an issue in our lives that we need to work to resolve. If we are constantly stressed about finances, then financial health needs to be something we strategize and prioritize. If we are in constant conflict in our relationships, then learning emotional intelligence and how to better get along with others should be what we're focusing on.

Though most people allow life to happen to them, the emotionally resilient recognize that a lot of life is a reflection of them, and therefore, they can control their own outcomes.

Reform yourself.

Discomfort is a call to change.

When we are most uncomfortable in our lives, it is often because life is demanding a better version of us start showing up. Though discomfort seems as though it should be our enemy, it is really our greatest ally, a deep and pervasive knowing that we are deserving of more, capable of more, and destined for more.

The most impactful thing that emotionally resilient people do is adapt. When their old ways can no longer support them, they reinvent. They release old aspects of themselves, and build new ones. They are in a constant state of growth.

Though you cannot always control what you feel, you can control how you respond, and in that response, you can find your freedom.

TRUST *that* YOUR HEART KNOWS *the* TRUTH, EVEN *if* YOUR MIND CANNOT MAKE SENSE *of* IT

If there is nothing else in this world that you can trust, please know that your heart knows what is true. Your heart can sense what's right for you, what's on the path you were meant for. Your heart will know what's going to help you evolve and expand into the person you are longing to be, and it will know what's standing in the way of that as well.

The heart's communication is subtle.

It does not inform you of that truth through the voice in your head, but rather, the very quiet inklings at your core. Your mind will not be able to place these feelings, nor make sense of them. Your mind is dedicated to the path you have laid, the pieces of a life you built for a person you still believe you are. Your mind craves reason and certainty and structure and logic and clarity, and that is precisely what will cause the most resistance.

Love is not reasonable.

Callings are not certain.

Awakening releases structure.

Soul does not operate through logic.

Your mind has built safety through believing that there is only one path to walk, only one way of life to be experienced in a lifetime.

Your heart knows something much greater. It knows that you were meant to seek what makes you come alive, it knows that the gifts embedded in you could heal many others, and it knows exactly the person that you are meant to be, even if you can't imagine anything else right now.

Your heart goes slowly. It does not act impulsively or irrationally or with anger. The heart shows you what is true through the feelings that do not fade. The heart shows you where you're meant to be by where it keeps bringing you. The heart is comfortable taking leaps of faith, because it can feel what's on the other side. The heart is used to believing before it can see. The heart is the centermost part of who you are, and the truth that lives there is the one you are meant to follow.

The most important journey of your life is not the one where you find the willpower to press forward with a life you do not truly want, but rather, to dare greatly, to lay it all on the line, to step over the horizon, to leap and trust that the road will rise to meet you.

You may believe that it has been your rational mind that's gotten you where you are today, but it's truly been a thousand unknowns that have come to life, little feelings that you followed despite everything that told you not to, little urges that were calling you into an entirely different world—one you could not yet see, but inevitably knew would be true.

It may have taken you a while to see clearly, but your heart has known the entire time. The question is not will you follow it or not, but how long will you wait until you begin the life that you know is meant to be yours.

HOW TO GET *over* SOMEONE: *the* ULTIMATE GUIDE *to* RELEASING ATTACHMENTS, REINVENTING YOURSELF, *and* OPENING YOUR LIFE *to* NEW LOVE

Heartbreak is a hard thing, but it's not a forever thing, and you will experience a disproportionate amount of it when you're young—though of course, it can hit us just as hard at any phase of life.

While you're dating, you're most likely moving from relationship to relationship, working on finding the person with whom you'll stay long-term. You'll have to cope with not just one but often a string of losses and heartbreaks. The repetitiveness can begin to create a learned helplessness: it seems like your heart always gets broken, you never find the right person, or nobody is quite good enough for you. This is just a temporary thing.

Chances are, you will spend the rest of your life with someone whom you are happily coupled. You are not meant to be stuck in this back and forth. You are not designed to forge a beautiful connection with someone and then have it severed. You are not supposed to build foundations and then have someone crack them in half. This is why it feels so wrong, so foreign, and so awful: this is not how you're supposed to experience life, and it won't be how you experience life for the majority of your life.

Right now, the pain is making you feel like just because someone will be out of your life forever that the hurt will last forever too. But all you can see is what you've lost. You have yet to see what you're going to gain.

What is there to learn from heartbreak?

As it turns out, a lot.

Right now, life is offering you a second chance. It's telling you that the person you're hung up on is not the person you should be spending every day of your life with. Your life partner is someone who shapes you irrevocably. Their influence in your life will do a great deal in making you who you become. Is the person you are mourning the kind of person you want to be? Would you want to have kids just like them? If the answer is in any way no, you do not want to be with that person. In a few years, you'll look at them and want to fall to your knees with gratitude that you were rerouted.

Not that you feel that way right now.

Right now, you are so focused on what you think you have lost that you're not realizing the fertile ground that is in front of you. The earth shifts when our hearts break. When we are forced out of comfort, we transform. Right now, you have a choice: you can put all of your energy into throwing a hissy fit about not getting what you want, or you can take all of the energy that you were previously spending loving, caring, worrying, spending time with and thinking about this person, and you can put it into yourself.

Do you know what you can do when your energy is wholly your own?

Anything. Everything. You can start a side hustle and work until it becomes your main gig, and by this time next year, you could be self-employed doing what you love every day. You can take a trip to St. Tropez and sit on the beach alone. You can spend your nights reading and retaining knowledge that will literally change the entire quality of your life for decades to come. You can spend the money you were wasting on drinks and food and accommodations and start paying off your debts so you have fewer responsibilities and more freedom.

You can become exactly who you want and are meant to be. You have the rest of your life to be in love. You have right now to change yourself.

You're mourning the loss of a potential future—but it was just that, a potential.

It is normal and healthy to grieve the loss of someone with whom you used to have a deep or intimate relationship.

But when it becomes obsessive to the point of being devastated and completely incapable of moving on, it is no longer the person you are mourning, it is an idea you had about your future life.

When you break up with someone and mourn the loss of their presence in your lives, it's normal to feel lonely, for emotions to come in waves, to cry, to want to avoid them or start over or take some time for yourself. But when you break up with someone on whom you were in some way relying on to give you a sense of certainty, direction or security for the future, the reaction will be much more manic. You'll be obsessive, convinced that it's not the end, desperately looking for "signs," doing anything to make them believe you are still meant to be together.

That kind of reaction is not the reaction of someone who has loved and lost a person they care about. That is the kind of reaction of someone who has lost a feeling of safety about the future and will go to any length to get it back...even just believing in their own minds that it's "not over." In that, you are giving yourself that feeling again.

Here's a litmus test for you: what was going on in your life when you first got together with this person? Before you were in this relationship, did you know where your life was going? Were you confident in who you were, what you wanted, and how you were planning to proceed with the next few years of your life? Were you at all worried, stressed or anxious that you hadn't found a relationship by the "right time," or that you'd hit some milestone and be alone? Were you feeling lost in your career, stressed about money, or tense about your family?

The circumstances that existed when the relationship began can tell you so much about the relationship itself. This is why people preach from the gospel of "Love Yourself First" so often: when two people who are happy, well adjusted, and pursuing their own individual goals get together, the relationship lasts. When two people who need self-work get together, they use one another as a Band-Aid, and then it falls apart because ultimately, they realize: another person is not a solution.

If you are anxious about the future, you need to be the one to make a plan. If you feel unsure about what you want, you need to sit down and brainstorm until you come up with some ideas. If you don't know who you are, you need to do some soul-searching. If you feel unfulfilled, you need to work somewhere new. If you feel stressed, you need to manage your time, money or relationships better.

This is what you needed to do then, and it is what you are getting a chance to do now.

You're not going to forget about this person. You're going to have to get distracted.

"Forgetting" about someone is impossible. The more you try not to think about them, the more you will. Carrying on with your days like nothing has changed is not what it's going to take to "move on" with your life. The normal that you once knew is gone. If you keep trying to live as though this person is still around, you will be orbiting around empty spaces. It will be impossible to not think of them and mourn for them constantly. You will sit in the room you used to sit in together and cry. You'll visit the store you use to shop in together and feel defeated. You'll see the friends you used to hang out with and sense embarrassment because in a very public way, you failed.

You need to get up, you need to start over, and you need to begin anew. You need new places, people, and routines. You need new adventures and goals and plans.

This is how you get over anything: you fill your life with so many powerful, world-altering things that slowly, over time, you begin to think about them less and less. Not because you're trying to, but because you have so many other things to think about now. You have so many places to go, things to hope for, and passions to keep your mind consumed.

As time goes on, you'll think about that person less and less and less. Not because you magically stopped caring about them one day, but because you started filling your life with things you cared about more.

That, right there, is the magic of heartbreak: it forces you to be a different person. Unless you want to mourn forever, you have to change. And if you do it right, you'll work on becoming the person you always wanted to be. You'll look back on this moment as the pinnacle, the turning point, the unanswered prayer that was the answer itself. It will be the greatest thing that ever happened to you because instead of a lukewarm relationship that wasn't working anyway, you got the life of your dreams... and you were the one who gave it to yourself.

How do you know when someone is actually right for you?

The tricky thing about relationships is that they almost never end with certainty. It's not obvious that you should or shouldn't be with this person. For every issue that you have, you could list off all of their redeeming qualities. For every argument, you could rattle off all the great times you had together, all the signs and signals and ways you're positive that you're just "meant to be."

The opposite of knowing someone is right for you isn't being sure someone is wrong for you.

The opposite of knowing someone is right for you is being *overwhelmingly uncertain.*

When someone is clearly and overwhelmingly "wrong" for you, your relationship won't get that far. You won't be able to develop and foster any kind of significant connection. You'd realize that you are fundamentally incompatible long before you could form any kind of attachment. This is not how heartbreak happens. It is not the product of being mismatched with someone who is fundamentally "wrong."

It is being matched with someone who in many ways could be "right," but raises just as many doubts. Realizing that someone is wrong for you happens in tiny gestures. It is not posting a lot of photos online, because somewhere deep down, you know the relationship isn't going to last. It's avoiding introducing them to your parents, because you know they aren't going to react as well as you'd hope. It's thinking to yourself in quiet moments, "But what if there's something else?" It's daydreaming about the possibilities that life could hold if you weren't with that person.

It's going back and forth wondering if this is the person you could spend your life with, rather than just being in the moment each day and actually spending your life with them.

Heartbreak doesn't happen with people who are wholly wrong for you. You aren't able to get close enough to let it hurt. It happens with people who are just right enough to make you hope, but just wrong enough to prevent you from getting closer, or making it official.

That's why you don't have to watch out for the people who reject you as much as you do the people who leave you hanging, the people who keep wanting to see you without making a commitment, the people who say it's "just not the right time" or that they "aren't looking for anything serious." The truth is that nobody is looking for anything serious until someone comes along who they seriously love. It is never the right time until it is the right person.

The opposite of "just knowing" someone is right for you isn't "just knowing" they are wrong for you. It's doubt. Being very uncertain means you know the answer...you are just too attached to admit it.

How do you "let go" when you can't stop thinking about someone?

In the wake of your breakup, everyone around you is going to be counseling you to just "let go" of the past, move on, and start anew. They'll tell you to go out drinking, start dating, and revel in your newfound freedom. This will be annoying at best, and absolutely maddening at worst. There's nothing more frustrating than someone who seems to believe that a shot of tequila and a random Saturday hookup will be a salve for the life-shattering heartbreak you're experiencing right now. The future as you thought it would be has changed. The present as you're used to it has, too. You do not need any more uncertainties right now. You do not need to try to force yourself into a new life when you're already panicked about what's going to happen next.

The harder you try to "let go" and "move on," the more your brain is going to latch onto reasons why you should think about it more, try again, or keep hoping.

The thing about "letting go" is that it's less an active choice as it is accepting that something is already gone. It's not really that you actually dismiss someone from your life, it's that you come to terms with the fact that they are already gone. In that, you can find a semblance of peace: you aren't toying with whether or not you should unclasp your hand and release something, you only have to realize that you are already living without this person. They are already gone. You have, essentially, already let go.

People feel uncertainty because it's the unknown. But uncertainty is also an incredible blessing, because it means that for the first time, you are detached from what happened in the past and what you think you want to happen in the future. When you are uncertain, you are open to making choices that otherwise wouldn't have been possible, because you were too comfortable with what you were used to. Uncertainty is a breeding ground for life's greatest moments and most epic possibilities.

Most people hang onto what they've known and what they think they want because they are too afraid of feeling the discomfort of not knowing. People who are willing to brave that tension are the ones who truly free themselves.

The ground rules for moving on from a relationship:

When you're hurt and uncomfortable and desperately wanting to retrace your steps, figure out what went wrong or even try to mend things again, you're going to be in a place in which you are not thinking clearly. Call it a crime of passion, but people are most apt to completely embarrass themselves and make detrimental decisions for their long-term wellbeing when they're most in emotional pain. That's why if you're going through a split, you should follow these guidelines:

01 | Follow a no-contact policy, unless the relationship wasn't that serious and you're comfortable being friends again. Exes don't hang out alone, go out for drinks, or talk to each other regularly... and they certainly don't hook up.

02 | Find a trustworthy friend to whom you can vent, and do so privately.

03 | If you can't help but feel the urge to check in on them, to view their photos or to see what they're doing online, unfriend or block them. If you feel bad doing that, explain kindly that it's a step for you to gain closure and to help you move on, and that you wish them well.

04 | **Switch up your routine.** You cannot hang out with the same people, visit the same places, and otherwise continue to circle in orbit around them and not expect to miss them every minute of the day. When you go through a breakup, your whole life changes...that's the magic of it.

05 | **Don't do anything permanent.** Don't do anything you cannot undo in a matter of days.

06 | **Consider casually dating again.** After you've taken some time for yourself, consider getting back in the game. No, it's not fair to enter a new relationship hung up on someone else. But if you are never really going to forget your old relationship until you have a new one to take its place and remind you that everything happens for a reason.

07 | **Write down everything that you wanted and needed this person to be for you.** Most likely, you're scared because without them, your future could be lonely, financially harder, or you might just feel like a total screw up. Those are all issues that you need to work on mending for yourself. A relationship is not a Band-Aid. Treating it like one is what landed you with the wrong person in the first place.

08 | **Remember that all you are losing is one idea you had about what your future might have been.** You're now free to start dreaming of a new one.

How "future self" work can help you heal:

Future self work is a process of visualizing yourself many years down the line. When you sit down to do it, make sure you're in a quiet and calm place, and have a pen and paper handy. Close your eyes and visualize the highest and best version of your future self. It doesn't matter what age you are. Know that it is common to first see scary things (like being dead or hurt or in pain when you're older) and know that it is just your fear of what could happen that you're seeing.

Once that subsides and you can finally see what you're going to be like in the future, start asking that person questions, and see what they say in your mind. Know that this is all entirely a projection of who you already are and where you already know you're meant to be heading... it's just a process of making you aware of that fact.

Often, visualizing yourself happy and single or happy and coupled with someone new in the future is just what you need to let go of someone. Your future self could also advise you on what to do in the moment, or whether or not you really need to let a relationship go. You are basically tapping into the counsel of the highest and wisest part of yourself (future self = older, which means, better developed) and as long as what you write down feels real, true and helpful, you should trust it.

The reality is that you already are that best version of yourself. Everything that's happening around you right now is helping you to realize that once and for all.

IF YOU EVER FEEL LOST, *please* REMEMBER *that you* CAN MAKE *a* HOME *within* YOUR OWN HEART

You were never meant to find a permanent home in a temporary world.

Other people were never meant to love you into a feeling of safety and security.

You are here to make a home within your own heart. You are here to learn not that you don't need connection, but that without being connected to yourself, nothing else is viable. You are here not to burrow yourself into a life someone else built, but to find the courage to create your own.

Your chest is where peace is.

Your heart is where love is.

Your mind is where inspiration is.

The people who walk along with you on the journey are never to be taken for granted, but they are also never to be utilized for your own emotional labor.

It is nobody else's job to make us feel safe, to make us feel that all is well and right.

Until you are at home in your own heart, you will never make peace with the world.

This is because you will be constantly requiring things to be different than they are, constantly needing people to fulfill your own expectations of them, constantly needing to weave around your fears and your triggers.

What you have to realize instead is that home is not an idea, it's not a place, it's a way of being.

It's a way you show up to your life and make it your own.

It's a way you find comfort in the contours of who you are, not who you might one day become.

It's the way you seek presence in all things, to realize that nothing is meant to be perfect, but everything is a new experience that you didn't have before, and might never have again.

Making a home within yourself is knowing you will always be okay not because everything will go the way you initially planned, but because you will adapt even if it doesn't.

Making a home within yourself is knowing that you will always move forward not because it won't be hard to let go, but because you can do hard things.

Making a home within yourself is knowing that you will always return to peace, not because you will always be comfortable, but because you are willing to feel uncomfortable in order to have the life you've asked for.

We are not alive to coast.

We are not alive to seek safe spaces within the idea of another.

We are here to realize that we are the source of our own existence, of all that we create, of all that we are.

We are here to bring ourselves home, and then to show others the way back to themselves.

16 LITTLE REMINDERS *for when* YOU FEEL LIKE YOU AREN'T QUITE *where you* WANT *to be* IN LIFE

You have come so far.

Please think about where you were a year ago, or three, or five, or seven. You have scaled mountains, you have overcome things you once thought would you never would. You have done things you did not think you could do, even if some of those were just getting out of bed and facing another day.

You can live within the questions.

Life doesn't start when we're set on the answers, it unfolds within the questions themselves. It's not knowing where we're going to end up, but the journey of exploration and soul-searching and deep-diving and connecting and seeking and ultimately arriving at our north. It's not always knowing exactly what we'll be doing in 10 years, but having the courage to pursue what feels right and comes effortlessly today. It's not always being certain that one relationship is the end-all, be-all of your existence, but showing up to it each day in spite of the unknown. *Certainty is the cheap way out.* It's giving a final answer when you're meant to unravel the question until the answer is a piece of you—so obvious, and so present, something you do not need to decide, but simply choose to embrace.

You're not behind.

You're not off-track. There is no way to be. Your life is a continuous unfolding of yourself. It is shaped and guided by the world outside of you, and how you interpret and respond to that world. It's an ongoing exploration of who you are and how you might be. Life does not begin when everything is perfect. It does not start when you think you're worthy. It's happening right now. You are not anywhere but where you are supposed to be, because there is nowhere else to be. The idea that you might have to earn your way into the life that is already yours is an illusion.

Life isn't a linear ascent into perfection.

When you're watching a movie, you don't spend the whole hour and a half just waiting for the ending, for the final answers. You understand that each piece of the story has meaning, each part is there to be enjoyed, savored, metabolized. You don't expect all of the strings to pull together and for everything to make sense right away, but you remain curious, you observe, you interpret and predict and you stay the course. Your life is the same way. You're living in a work of art while treating it as an equation that you have not yet solved. We do not create ourselves once and then never again, we are a lifelong project, an ever-shifting, continual blossoming.

Nobody expects as much of you as you do of yourself.

I know this is so hard to believe. I know you imagine that everyone you come across is evaluating your successes and failures, mapping them through their minds and arriving at a conclusion about the light through which they'll see you. I want to tell you a secret: *that light is your own.* That is the perception you're projecting, that is the lens you're seeing *yourself* through. The brain is a funny thing in that it's primary goal is to feel affirmed, and often when our most pronounced fears about ourselves take the center of our consciousness, we end up seeking reasons to believe in them more, not less. The point is that you don't know how other people see you, you're not in their minds. You can only know how you imagine yourself to be, and then consider for a moment that you don't spend much time evaluating every detail of someone else's existence, and so maybe (just maybe) you are likewise at the center of your own universe.

Weaving through the shadows is part of the experience.

Facing the hardships is part of the experience. There is no experience through which you cannot seep out a part of your soul that was once a mystery to you. That, in itself, is part of the magic.

You don't have to be certain.

Almost anything that truly calls your soul will take you off the certain and consistent path that a million others have carved out of the unknown. It's never going to be reasonable to travel, or pursue art, to love the person you love. There will always be a reason not to, another thing you could or should or might be doing with your time. Sometimes, in an effort to make sense of our lives, we end up more lost than ever because love isn't logical, joy isn't logical, passion isn't logical. You have to find the courage to paint outside the lines you once drew for yourself.

You have to start being kind to yourself.

Kind in the way that you're kind to a child, to someone or something so innocent and endlessly deserving of your affection and praise. We have to be kindest to ourselves when it seems least deserved, because that's usually when it is most needed. Find the simplest and most obvious ways to do that. Over time, you will find that so much of the relentless internal pressure are voices you once heard and then took as your own.

You probably don't need as much as you think you do.

You do not need a lot to be successful, you do not need to be a lot to be enough. You do not need a lot to be content, fulfilled, and happy. You do not need as much as you think you do, and widening that gap in the name of ambition will not make you reach for more, it will only leave you emptier. Know what you need, know what you want, and draw a line in the sand. You cannot spend the entirety of your life desperately and exhaustedly seeking. You must make time to simply be.

The fullest expression of your potential isn't about quantity, but quality.

Being loved means being completely seen and embraced by a few close people, not seeing just how many people you can convince to admire you. Being successful does not mean making as much money as possible, but being able to wake up every day and feel grateful to be alive, even in spite of all you've been through, even in spite of the fear. It is not how much you have, but how much what you have makes you believe life is worth living. It is not about how far you might climb from yourself, but whether or not you settle in.

It's normal to be uncomfortable.

Discomfort is a beautiful messenger. Unlike its sister signal, pain, discomfort often points us toward where we are most primed for growth, whereas hurt points us toward where we can no longer grow. Discomfort is what quietly communicates to us that something isn't quite right, which means that deep down, we know there is an alternative path, even if we're afraid to embrace it completely. Discomfort is your friend, not your enemy, and asking it what it has arrived to tell you is the only way to coexist with it, otherwise you end up constantly at war within yourself.

Big things happen in small steps.

You might be thinking that the problem with your life is the lack of big, breakthrough moments, momentus achievements and distinguishable exits from the past and entries into a new and more glamorous life. You might be thinking the problem isn't that you don't live in the coolest city, or that you're not the most well-respected individual in your field, or that some-one else has more than you which means you're simply not doing enough. The truth is that big things happen in small parts. It's not about those one-off changes, it's about the ac-cumulation of intentions you set day-in and day-out. You are far more defined by your daily routine than you are whether or not you moved someplace in particular or accomplished something in particular all by an equally particular point in time. The truth is that the path will lead you to where you need to be inevitably—holding your breath until you arrive only delays you getting there.

Nobody has it all figured out.

Part of the story that occurs in our minds that makes us be-lieve we aren't quite keeping up pace with our peers is this idea that everyone else has it figured out. How couldn't we think that? Look at the endless stream of their accomplishments and moves and family photo-shoots we see non-stop. How couldn't it appear as though everyone has it completely together and we are just scrambling to stay where we are? The highlight reel can be deceiving. We aren't supposed to know every detail and milestone of every person we've ever been acquaintances with since childhood. This is an experience that's distinctly unique to the digital age, and it's one we're still adapting to. Before the internet, you'd move on from a place or a school or a group and you'd actually move on, not stay gently connected despite being geographically, mentally and emotionally in different worlds. It's tricking you into thinking everyone you've ever known has it together, and you don't. It's just not so.

You're right on pace for the life that is yours.

The truth is that right here, right now, right as you are—you are right on time. You are running on schedule. There is no way you *couldn't* be, because there is no wrong way to move through the path that is your own life. When we are too certain of what's next in life, it is often because we are following someone else's path.

The journey isn't about convincing yourself that you're enough, but loving yourself even if you aren't.

On the road to believing that you're enough for this life, you will begin by trying to seek out evidence that disproves your worst fears. Of course, if you are sought after to date, you are appealing, and so you are worthy. Of course, if you get into your dream school, you are smart enough for your future, and so you are worthy. Of course, if you are liked by many, social proof says you're a amicable person, and so you're worthy. Unfortunately, life doesn't actually work this way, because even when we gather all of those reasons we should believe in our worth, we really don't feel it until we decide to love ourselves *even if we don't believe we're worth it.* Instead of trying to convince yourself that you're the best person ever, try instead just caring for yourself and your surroundings unconditionally. Worth is not something we earn, but something we remember as we cultivate our own care and approval.

You are doing better than you think you are.

You are closer to a breakthrough than you believe. You have come farther than you remember. You are doing better than you think, because your brain and body is hardwired to constantly focus on the next problem, the next threat, the next fear. This is meant to keep you safe, when really, it slowly fractures your heart. It makes you believe that nothing you accomplish is enough, that you are destined to live the rest of your life leaping from one high to the next, always bracing for the inevitable crash. *Even if all you did today was keep breathing,* you did enough. You are not only as worthy as you prove yourself to be. Your worth is a self-evident byproduct of the presence of your being. Maybe the point is that you stop and finally feel it.

WHEN LIFE GIVES YOU *an* OPPORTUNITY *to* CHANGE, PLEASE *don't* LET IT PASS YOU BY

When life offers you the opportunity to change course, you should take it.

You should take it because what ends up on our doorstep is almost always what's meant for us, even if we didn't anticipate its arrival. You should take it because the number of opportunities you'll be given to deeply change your life are far fewer than you think. You should take it because just the hunch that you should is an indicator that you want to.

But more than anything else, you should take it because when life gives us an opportunity to change, it's almost always because change is needed.

It's easy to romanticize what's comfortable. It's normal to prefer what's familiar. You've spent so much time convincing yourself that where you are is where you want to be, you've extolled every virtue and sought every explanation to justify why you need to stay precisely where you are.

But all of that mental chatter might be clouding your vision.

When you have to try so hard to convince yourself that something is right, it's almost always because deep down, you know that something is wrong.

When we're on the right path, it simply is.

We don't have to do mental gymnastics to convince ourselves that we're in the right place at the right time. It's just obvious, and even if doubt does creep in now and again.

Sometimes, we get caught in the grey area for a while.

We find ourselves stuck between knowing we're outgrowing where we are, and yet not seeing the next stone to leap on. If we're not mindful, the opportunity that we're craving might just pass us by, because our focus is too fixed, too shortsighted.

Giving into life is trusting life.

It's believing that there are no wrong turns, there are only turns, and how we make one after the next. It's understanding that though there are often serendipities too strong to seem coincidental. It's realizing that the world will not punish or reward us for one arbitrary choice over another, it's only a matter of how we pursue what's in the deepest alignment with who we are, how we are or aren't able to express our truth in the fullest.

We are not here to just play by the rules.

We were not born to just hit milestone after milestone.

We do not exist to run on someone else's script.

We are here to witness our souls in action, we are here to bring the world within us out into the world around us.

We are here to explore, to play, to try, to seek, to discover, to learn, to grow, to change, to adapt, to feel the highest highs and lowest lows and everything in-between.

The only thing we aren't here for is staying still.

When life gives you an opportunity to change, when a fork opens up in the road, when the detour becomes the destination, when you're given something greater than you'd know to ask for—it's not a coincidence.

One day, you'll look back and the steps will add up to a path that is clear.

One day, you'll realize that you received what you needed, even if it isn't always what you wanted.

One day, you'll understand that failure is not taking a misstep, it's never going anywhere beyond your current place because you are so afraid to get it wrong.

When life gives you an opportunity to change, give yourself the chance to get it right.

ON *the* DAYS
it FEELS LIKE
YOU'LL NEVER
MOVE FORWARD,
just REMEMBER *how*
FAR YOU'VE COME

On the days when it feels like you will never get through this season, this period, this transition—please remember all of the mountains you have scaled before. Please remember all of the nights you spent convinced that the anxiety wouldn't leave, that you'd never move beyond where you were in that very moment.

Whether you realized it or not, the time passed. Without you having to even try, joy emerged from your days. One day, something small brought you a little ease, and then a little more. You waited. You realized that everything was going to be okay, even if it doesn't always feel okay. You let the waves crash, and then you let them recede.

Whether you realized it or not, you found courage. You did things you once did not believe you could do, even if those things were just finding the will to wake up and face each day. You felt worse than you were capable of feeling, you suffered loss that you couldn't have conceived prior. You were awakened to reality, which is sometimes cold, and sometimes hard, and sometimes brutally unfair.

But also unimaginably sweet. Because while you were mourning what you thought would be, you also found softness. You discovered how important it is to love the people nearest to you, and how invaluable they are. You began to appreciate what you didn't see before. You began to know that you were enough, because you decided what was enough.

Whether you realized it or not, you became resilient. You explored the perimeters of what your heart could hold, and how much it could process. You discovered that your strength is limitless, you just don't know what if it's never been tested before.

And over time, what was once impossible became easy.

The life you have today is a mere dream of the past. The things you do right now were once the things you only could have ever prayed to have. The people in your life are the ones you gazed out the window for years and wondered if they would ever arrive, if someone would ever show up that made you feel so deeply understood.

You do not have to have everything in order to make the best of anything, because goodness is something we choose to see. It's not always something we can achieve, or find.

So when the day comes that it feels most like you will never move beyond where you are right now, please remember how far you have walked, and through what. Please remember all of the times you were stuck and were sure you would never get out from under the crushing weight of your own disappointment and defeat. Please remember all of the times you were truly heartbroken, truly let down.

Then remember all of the nights you dreamed of being where you are right now. The days you spent working and planning and hoping that it would all work out. In one way or another, a path was made where it did not exist before. The opportunities showed up. The doors creaked open. You met the people who you'd spend years of your life with, people who were once strangers.

You discovered things about yourself you did not yet know. You learned what it takes to feel safe, and not. You learned what you enjoy, and what you don't. You learned what you value, and what you don't. Because you discovered, you learned the honest truth of who you are and who you're going to be.

You found yourself, not because you were searching, but because you were cornered. When discomfort in life peaks, we are left to look around and wonder why. Through that reflection, we discover all the pieces that are out of place, and then we find the courage to put them back together.

You will move the pieces in front of you today.

You will arrive at the horizon you're gazing at in due time.

Instead of fearing that the road will fall out from under you, return to what life has shown you: that things can be scary, but that a way is always made. That even if you don't believe you're worthy, you're always given enough. That even if you don't believe you're lovable, you're always loved. That even if you don't think there's a way forward, there always is.

When it feels most like nothing will ever give and the mountain ahead of you won't ever be scaled, remember how you crossed every one that's behind you: one step, one hour, one moment, one glimmer of hope at a time.

10 THINGS YOU WILL START *to* FEEL *when a* BIG LIFE CHANGE *is around the* CORNER

Sometimes when our lives are about to change, we can sense it before we can see it. These are a few of the experiences you might have right before a massive shift takes place.

01 | You'll stop pretending like everything is fine.

When we're really stuck in life, denial is the shield we use to protect ourselves from the panic of acknowledging everything that's wrong because we don't yet have the confidence to believe we can fix it.

When we're approaching a big life change, what we're really coming up on is the tipping point at which we are finally ready to reconcile what's been "off" for a pretty long time.

This means that you're going to be phasing out of the denial period, and into anger, regret, remorse, and even sadness.

These are feelings you've had pent up for a really long time, that you probably feel safe enough to release now because you know the story is changing, your life is adjusting as it really needed to be all along.

We don't snap out of denial one day, we slowly come out of it in phases, and eventually, we accept that we weren't happy before.

02 | You'll look back at the choices that led you to where you are.

Big life changes are often a time for reflection.

It's when we realize that we're moving from one chapter to the next that we often stop to take stock of what happened in our story prior, and how that contributed to where we are now.

More than anything, we start to become more self-aware.

We begin to recognize why we ended up where we did. We begin to think about the choices that led us to where we currently stand, and how we might need to choose differently if we want a different outcome in the future.

Whether you're proud of what you've done or regretful, this reflection process gleans a lot of important wisdom for moving forward.

03 | You'll get clear on what you really want.

The process of getting out of denial is also the process of getting into alignment.

When you acknowledge what you do not want, you cannot help but identify its opposite: what you do want.

You might discover that realizing what you want is not an inspiring process. Quite the opposite, in fact.

You might arrive at these conclusions from a place of anger, regret, and total exasperation. You might realize that you've been denying yourself even the ability to recognize what you want, let alone pursue it wholeheartedly.

Regardless of how you arrive, what's important is that you can no longer neglect what you truly desire, and that's a good thing, even if it's uncomfortable in the process.

04 | You'll shed everything that you no longer want to carry.

You might find yourself physically releasing what's around you.

You might clean out your closet and the clothes that no longer suit you, you might go through your belongings and do a deep purge. You might change where you live, stop talking to some friends and connect with others, and so on, and so forth.

This is a subconscious way of making your outer world align with what's happening throughout your inner world.

Deep down, you know you're moving on, and you can't do so with all of the weight of the past keeping you stuck.

05 | You'll address other long-standing issues.

When you heal one part of your life, it tends to radiate out and touch all of the others.

Maybe you're getting out of denial regarding the city you're living in, or the type of work that you do, or the long-term viability of a relationship. In the process, you might find yourself wanting to address other things that have been bothering you for a long time.

When we improve or elevate one part of our lives, the others that remain unhealed begin to stand out more starkly in comparison.

Just remember to take it one thing at a time and not totally overwhelm yourself.

You can both acknowledge what needs to change while doing it at a safe pace.

06 | Things will start to come full circle.

With all of this revelation and change happening, you might find yourself having a "full circle" ending.

Maybe you kind of always had a hunch about what you're doing now. Maybe you're accepting parts of yourself that have existed all along, though you've been in denial of them.

Maybe you're realizing that you kind of always, deep down, knew what you know now, even though you tried to avoid it. Maybe you're finally coming to terms with what you wanted all along.

Maybe you can remember yourself saying: I always wanted to live there.

Maybe you are finally realizing that the work that comes most effortlessly to you is always what you were meant to be doing.

Maybe you are recognizing that you knew your relationship was a dead end from the very beginning, but you pursued it anyway.

No matter what's shifting or what revelations are occurring, you might find that you're sort of ending where you started, and it's really more comforting than you'd imagine.

07 | You'll rediscover your sense of self.

A natural side effect of recognizing what you do and do not want in your life is likewise realizing who you are and are not.

In this process, you might find that you're discovering a stronger, and clearer, sense of self.

You know what you want, you know what you're good at, you know what you want to experience.

You're adjusting who you are on the outside to better reflect who you know you are on the inside, and it's a bittersweet process. While it can be a pretty hard ego-hit to accept that you haven't been the person you want to be, it's quickly released in favor of the feeling of finally being true to yourself, which is invaluable and irreplaceable.

You're realizing that you're worthy of the life you want, and you have always been.

08 | You'll start to get a glimpse of inner peace.

Through all the periods of clearing stored emotions, getting out of denial and embracing who you are, you'll find that glimpses of deep, inner peace are becoming more normal.

This will be different than being excited or energized, because this sense is really the feeling that you're finally where you're supposed to be, not anxious that you'll never arrive, or that you don't deserve to.

You're starting to sense that you're showing up in the moment the way you want to be, and it's a life-changing realization to have.

09 | You'll start to have long-term clarity.

The funny thing about figuring out what you want in the moment is that it often lends itself to the bigger picture, too.

You might find yourself realizing what you want long-term, or what your life might look like. This might have been completely foreign to you just a short while ago, but now that you're becoming more comfortable with who you are and what you want, it's easier to see ahead, and that's something you take additional comfort in.

10 | You'll let go with gratitude, and step in with grace.

Periods of transition can be tough, but when you're really ready, you'll know how to let go with gratitude, and step in with grace.

What this means is that you'll be thankful for everything you've experienced, including each misstep and mistake. From each, you learned something invaluable, and for that, you won't really regret it.

Then you'll step in with that same sense of appreciation. You'll take the first strides into your new chapter with a feeling of ease and awe, because you know what it's like to live out of alignment with who you are—and you'll never forget how good it feels to finally be on the other side.

THERE'S NO SUCH THING *as* FALLING BEHIND, *there is* NOT *just one* WAY YOUR LIFE CAN UNFOLD

Here is a sentence that will either disrupt your worldview or free you, and probably both: *Everybody is having the exact experience that they need to be having right now.*

This is hard to accept when we see people around us making what we perceive to be grave errors in their lives.

This is hard to accept when we witness the people we love struggling and we want to show them the way out.

This is hard to accept when we can't stop judging and punishing ourselves for not being better, farther, and different.

When we are young, and before we really have a sense of autonomy, our lives are governed by a process, a specific order.

We know that we learn to crawl then walk.

We know that we learn to tie our shoes and put on our jackets.

We know that when we're done with 2nd grade, we go to 3rd.

Our lives are built-in reinforcing systems.

We are reinforced by our peers, by our family, by our grades.

We know that the goal is to graduate, pursue a job or an education, get married, and have kids.

Then, of course, life happens.

We find that this one formula for an existence is just really a suggestion, one to guide us toward prosperity and not self-destruction.

We aren't often given a lesson on how to be fulfilled.

We aren't often told what to do if we don't quite get there when everyone else does, if our big milestones are letdowns, or most commonly, if we check off every box on the list and find that we are, somehow, still empty inside.

Falling behind is an illusion.

There is no such thing.

There is not one way for your life to unfold.

Sometimes, we have to take the back road because the long way around teaches us what we need to know.

Sometimes, we sit in our own pain for years before we start waking up and adjusting our behavior.

Sometimes, what we learn from being different is more important than what we'd learn from fitting in.

Sometimes, our greatest successes are decades in the making.

Sometimes, we do peak early.

Sometimes, we need years of growth and self-discovery to decide what we need next. Sometimes, the point of the journey is to have different experiences, not just to cycle through a series of them until we decide on the one thing we want forevermore.

When we believe that it is possible to fall behind, we place limits on our lives.

When we believe that it is possible to fall behind, it is because we think that the point of life is just to arrive at a certain series of checkpoints...until we die.

Graduate, get a job, pay the bills, mildly hate yourself, get married, fight with your spouse, have kids, fight with them, grow old, retire...and then try to enjoy what's left.

If you are truly worried about falling behind your peers, please ask yourself what you really think you're falling behind on.

So many people met every single milestone they were meant to and are no happier for it.

This is because life is not about just going through the motions.

Life is meant to be lived.

Life is meant to be experienced.

And we often find that our pain is the portal to awakening to that experience.

Discomfort is the signal that there's more for us, there's more to savor, more to feel, to be.

What if you did not measure your life by how it compared to who is around you, but instead how it felt inside of you?

What if your priority wasn't on the type of growth that people can see, but the type of personal growth that revolutionizes you, the kind that changes the way you do everything from sipping your coffee in the morning to breathing in spring air.

Sometimes, the setback is the journey.

Because the path you were on wasn't going somewhere you wanted anyway.

Sometimes, the setback is the wake-up call you need to save your life.

Because otherwise, you were barreling toward your own self-destruction.

Sometimes, being different isn't a bad thing.

It means you're on a journey of something deeper, and something bigger, that most people wouldn't even dare to dream of.

THIS IS HOW
YOU WILL KNOW
if you're ACTUALLY
on the WRONG
PATH *in* LIFE

Sometimes, it isn't always clear that we are on the wrong path in life until we are too far down it to easily turn around.

We have all had an experience like this at least once before.

We spent years engaging in self-damaging behaviors only to wake up one day and finally see what we were doing to ourselves. We dug ourselves into deep debt mindlessly, only to pay the consequences later. We spent years in a relationship that had an expiration date, and we were sidelined to discover we had invested so much of our lives into something that was only ever temporary.

Once we have an experience like this, it's easy to want to spend the rest of your life worrying that it may happen again, that you might wake up one day to find that one mistake after the next lead you to a place you didn't want to be.

You imagine that hypervigilance will take care of this—that if you think through it enough, and second-guess yourself often, maybe you'll be able to avoid the heartbreak.

Except you won't.

The absolute honest truth is that when you are actually on the wrong path in life you know the entire time—when you finally have no choice but to come to terms with it, you have the epiphany.

The honest truth is that if you are on the wrong path, you already know.

You knew what you were doing when you were engaging in self-destructive behaviors, there was no point in time at which you fooled yourself into thinking what you were doing was healthy or okay.

You knew what you were doing when you were getting into debt, you just had enough mental ammunition to keep justifying it and convincing yourself that it was the right thing to do.

You knew that your relationship was going to end, because you knew that it wasn't that good all along. *No good relationship ends in the first place,* why would it? We never leave people we truly love and value and care for. Relationships that end are relationships that need to end, and if we're honest with ourselves, the signs were there all along.

The point is that you don't ever lose your moral compass, you just talk yourself out of it at times in order to serve yourself best.

Your innate understanding of right and wrong never really goes away, it just gets clouded by fear, by attachment, by the idea that what's in front of you is the best you may ever have.

Your acknowledgement that self-destructive behaviors are bad for you is clouded by the fact that they bring you comfort, which you convince yourself means it is, somehow, justified.

Your understanding that you were getting into more debt than you could handle was covered by a bigger fear, which was whatever you believed you had to use it to pay for instead of getting real with yourself about the fact that you couldn't afford your lifestyle.

Your realization that you were in the wrong relationship was completely ignored because you were terrified of what the future might hold, and desperate to know that maybe, just maybe, this certain someone could be beside you while you figured it all out.

If you want to spend your life worrying that you're making mistakes, don't bother.

Deep down, you already know.

You already know that the job you're at isn't for you forever.

You already know that you need to clean up your game and get your act together.

You already know what the issues in your relationship are, and you already know whether or not you're willing to work through them.

You already know what you need to do, and what you don't.

You know it even if you want to pretend you do not know it, and the longer you do that, the more lost you're going to be.

Your "big mistakes" in life never occurred because you were blind to their consequences, they occurred because you deluded yourself into thinking it was the right thing to do when you knew it wasn't.

Getting honest with yourself is the best form of self-protection there is.

Give that to yourself, and go forward with faith, with knowing that you can trust yourself, because you are no longer going to lie to yourself—even if the truth is inconvenient.

YOU WILL START FEELING LIKE ENOUGH *when you* DECIDE *what is* ENOUGH *for* YOU

Nobody is going to come along one day and convince you that you're enough.

As much as you think that's what might happen, nobody is going to hand your own love to you. Nobody will, because nobody can.

There have been so many people who have loved you madly in this life, and yet, not one of them has been able to convince you that you're enough. Think of how many people have expressed the deepest affection and admiration for you over the years, certainly you can think of at least a few. Yet it didn't shift your perception of yourself, at least not for long.

That's because it's not supposed to.

Self-worth is an inside job.

You will start feeling like enough when you decide what is enough for you.

You will start feeling like enough when you start setting the standards for your life and then reaching to meet them.

You will start feeling like enough when you decide what kind of work is enough for you, how much money is enough for you, what kind of material belongings are enough for you, how many friendships are enough for you, and what kind of lifestyle is enough for you.

Through deciding what is enough for you on the outside, you will begin to discover what is enough for you on the inside.

What do you really need to feel good, to feel complete, and to feel worthy? Most people dig to find it isn't much, it's just a small switch that needs to be turned on.

That light is one of awareness, of gratitude, and consciousness. That one is looking around and seeing just how much you have and knowing that, in the end, you really wouldn't need much else to get by.

You've had less and you've laughed until you've cried.

You've had less and you've fallen in love.

You've had less and still the sun shined every morning.

It is not that you need more to feel like you are enough, but that you need to decide what is enough for you so that you can stop trying to win a make-believe competition in your mind.

When you decide what is enough for you, you will no longer feel as though you have to prove yourself to yourself.

You will be able to release yourself from the anxiety of wondering whether or not someone else thinks you're good enough for your own life—because that kind of thinking is the root of your insecurity to begin with.

When you are enough for you, other people's measures don't seem to matter that much.

When you are no longer seeing your life through other people's eyes, you get to see, and feel, and create, all that you find truly beautiful.

When you decide what is enough for you, you realize that you have always been worthy of your own life.

9 QUESTIONS
that will HELP
YOU MAKE *the*
MOST *of* EVERY DAY

Our lives are composed of days. They pile on, one after the next, and if we're honest, most of us would admit we don't use each one as well as we could.

Maybe you've tried to micromanage your time and force yourself into a robotic routine—but that only makes you feel more trapped. Instead, gently encourage yourself to make better use of your days by asking yourself the following questions.

What would my best self do today?

Envisioning the best version of yourself can be a powerful motivator. However, simply imagining that person is more challenging than it sounds. Once you've imagined them, it's difficult to turn that idealized person into something concrete.

Here's a better way to approach this exercise: Ask yourself what your best self would do with the day ahead. How would they use this time? Where would they go? What would they accomplish, and how?

You should know instinctively.

What's the best thing that could happen to me today?

By imagining what the best possible thing that could happen to us would be, we can prime ourselves to experience it. In this mindset, the best possible outcome is often the most likely outcome.

Maybe it's that you finally got a long, much-needed nap. Maybe it's that you enjoyed a quiet walk outside. Maybe it's that you finished a project and it wasn't as tiresome as you'd feared.

Figure out what your best possible outcome is from the onset. Keep it in mind throughout your day.

What can I do better today than yesterday?

Growth happens incrementally. We don't wake up one day and completely change our behavior. Instead, each day we focus on being just 1% better than we were the day before.

Think of one thing, however small it might be, that you may be able to do better today than yesterday. Perhaps it's how you relate to your partner or kids, stepping away from work at a reasonable hour, or cooking that meal you said you would. These micro-improvements will eventually change your life.

What small step can I take today to fix a big problem?

The biggest problems in our lives exist because they feel, or seem, unsolvable. In reality, they're just more complex or time-consuming to solve.

Ask yourself what steps you could take today to chip away at one of your biggest goals, or an issue that's bothering you. Perhaps it's a debt repayment, a relationship you want to improve, or your health and wellness.

Don't worry about fixing everything in 24 hours. Instead, worry about which minor shifts you can make with the day ahead. These shifts, small as they might be, have the potential to impact your life for years to come.

What must I get done today?

While we're imagining all of our long-term aspirations and the steps we'll take to reach them, we must not forget the essentials—the tasks we must accomplish today to make those far-off goals possible.

Attending to the essentials will allow you to prioritize correctly and stay on schedule. We can't do it all at once, but if we prioritize one thing at a time, we can get it all done sooner than we think.

What am I doing for the most important person in my life today?

Who is the most important person, or people, in your life? (Even if that person is you.)

What are you doing for them today? It doesn't have to be a massive sacrifice. It could be as simple as paying them a phone call, writing them a letter (or a long email), or cooking dinner because you know they have a lot on their plate.

What's something new I can try today?

Of course, humans never evolve if they don't take risks—and if we don't take a risk today, when will we?

Instead of aiming for monumental endeavors, consider something small you can change about your day or routine to open yourself up to a new experience you're not sure you'll like.

Listen to a new playlist, cook a new dish, text someone you haven't in a while, or attempt a new hobby. Pay attention to how you feel.

Will I remember this day a year from now?

The answer for most of us, most days, is no. And not only is this important to realize, it's also freeing.

Instead of worrying about whether we failed or succeeded, enjoyed ourselves or didn't, realizing that we probably will not remember this specific day—even in the immediate future—helps free us from a bit of the pressure to make it absolutely perfect.

What could I do to make this day memorable?

With that said, some days are more memorable than others. If we make a concerted effort to challenge ourselves or rewrite our story in a small but meaningful way, we can turn an ordinary day into one that has an impact for a long time to come.

THIS YEAR, *please* STOP FIGHTING BATTLES *you* CAN'T WIN

Please stop fighting battles you cannot win.

Please stop trying to shop your way into self-esteem. Please stop trying to convince people to love you when they have no intent to. Please stop worrying about problems you can't solve. Please stop arguing with people who don't care enough to hear you out.

In life, there are battles that we can win and battles that we can't. If this were a game and you knew the only outcome was an inevitable loss, you would never participate. So why do you continue to play these mind games with yourself in which the only possible outcome is a reduction of your quality of life?

When you worry about a problem that isn't yours to solve, you are fighting a battle that you cannot win. You're trying to overthink your way into controlling someone else's behavior. You're misattributing their choices to a judgment about who you are. Worse, you think that everyone else around you needs to be okay for you to feel stable. These are all choices that rob you of your autonomy and power. There is no conclusion to this other than that you become progressively more manic and controlling, and reduce yourself to the worst possible version of who you could be.

When you try to buy your way into self-esteem, you are fighting a battle you cannot win. You keep trying to pin the problem onto something else—you think you're one more apartment upgrade, one more great Instagram picture, one more outfit, or one more beauty procedure away from really being comfortable with yourself. You're placing your sense of self on something outside of you, something always just beyond your reach. Until you are willing to stay still and show up and feel worthy simply by offering your presence, nothing around you is going to make you feel better, it's only going to drive you farther away from yourself.

When you try to convince someone to love you, you are fighting a battle you cannot win. Love is a free flowing thing. If someone does not give it effortlessly, it is not worth pursuing. If you have gotten to the point where you are so desperate for the presence of someone who has shown you that they do not care, eventually you have to ask yourself what they are doing for you that you cannot do for yourself. Are they making you feel safe, giving you direction, making you feel wanted? Whatever it is, you have to start meeting that need in a way that's actually sustainable. Love you have to beg for is not love, it is attachment.

When you try to argue with people who have no intent of hearing you, you are fighting a battle you cannot win. No, of course you don't want to give up on anyone, but eventually you have to realize that all of the stress and energy you pour into trying to convince someone to think a way that they refuse to—even if it would be better for them long-term—is just your own energy wasted. If someone isn't willing to change, they aren't going to change, and nothing you say or do will amend that.

Eventually, you have to decide that you care enough about yourself to stop fighting battles that are unfair to you.

Eventually, you have to decide that you're not going to keep investing your time and energy into thoughts and people that are never going to give you anything back. Eventually, you have to stop yourself mid-spiral and admit defeat. When you realize that there is no way for you to win a battle that isn't yours to fight, you don't lose—you're freed.

THIS IS *what it* REALLY MEANS *to be* KIND *to* YOURSELF, BECAUSE *it's not* AS EASY AS YOU THINK

When we think of kindness, we often confuse it for niceness, and the two are not the same.

When we are being nice, we are being placid and non-responsive. We are not aggravating, we are not triggering, we are not pointing out anything important, we are not addressing what needs to be said. We are washing over our natural and essential reactions for the sake of not disrupting someone else's waters, even if in all honesty, that's exactly what they need.

We behave this way because it's not always our place to tell someone what they need to hear.

It is always our place to maintain that type of honesty with ourselves.

Being kind to yourself is often doing the thing you least want to do.

It is very often prioritizing your future needs over your current wants. It is awakening yourself to your destructive habits, it is recognizing your self-defeating patterns, it is learning how to self-heal, it is setting boundaries first with ourselves and then with others, it is recognizing our power and remembering how we have neglected to use it.

That is kindness.

Everything else is a distraction.

The kindest thing to do is not always the easiest thing to do.

It doesn't always come with a sweet smile and a comforting hand. It doesn't always soothe us to sleep. True kindness is a fire that wakes you in the night. It's a calling that you can't ignore. It's tough love, it's seeing reality for what it is. It is acceptance, it is choice, it is reclamation.

When we are truly being kind to ourselves, we are actually in a process of reparenting ourselves.

We are doing for ourselves what we always relied on others to do—and we are doing it for the sake of our long-term and overall wellbeing.

We are taking ourselves up on an opportunity to do what is right as opposed to what is easy. We are choosing to do what is important over what is yet another way to numb and cope with the discomfort.

When we start solving problems, the discomfort goes away.

Kindness is loving ourselves enough to do that.

It is believing in our potential enough to choose better. It is caring enough about ourselves that we decide we're going to stop accepting a life that's less than what we deserve. It is fighting for who we are, and who we might one day be.

There is nobody in the world who can show you the type of kindness that you can show yourself.

Yes, through understanding and empathy and compassion, and then through the unending commitment to see yourself to a type of life in which you can do what you were born to do, be who you were born to be, and create what it is your ultimate destiny to create.

You are meant for that.

The only thing you have to do now is decide whether you're going to choose it.

REMEMBER THAT EVERYTHING *will* FEEL IMPOSSIBLE *right before* A HUGE SHIFT *takes* PLACE

When we hit our breaking point and assume we are more lost than ever before, it's not because everything has spontaneously gone wrong.

The breakdown is not a singular event, it is a tipping point. It's the moment at which we can no longer stay in denial about what's really going on.

We arrive here because we can't remember the last time we felt good about our bodies, because we've had the same relationship problems for years, because the negative thought patterns that have been eroding us are finally holding us back just enough that we know it's time to let them go.

Though it feels uncomfortable on the surface, this is the life-changing magic that we've been waiting for. The breakdown is a breakthrough, we just haven't seen the other side of it yet.

At the core of a breakdown moment is actually an awakening. It's you realizing that your old ways can no longer carry you forward.

For all of those years that you hated yourself, you were not yet self-aware enough to realize that you deserved more than to live in a constant state of dislike. That's why you feel uncomfortable now.

For all of those years you've had relationship problems, you were not yet accountable enough to realize that you had to make a change if you wanted to see a change. That's why you feel uncomfortable now.

For all of those years you've had negative thoughts weighing you down, you did not yet love yourself enough to no longer tolerate your own bullying holding you back. That's why you feel uncomfortable now.

But in each of these cases is you waking up and recognizing that it's time for something bigger, something greater, and something more.

That impossible feeling isn't actually impossibility. It's your honest feelings finally surfacing because you are now strong enough to respond to them, and to heal.

Everything will feel the most impossible right before a huge shift occurs.

Everything will seem the most hopeless right before the breakthrough happens.

Everything will feel as though it is falling apart right before it comes together.

It's so counterintuitive, but when we are most uncomfortable and lost is exactly when we're finally setting ourselves up to make the massive life change we've needed.

When we are finally ready to truly acknowledge and metabolize everything that's been holding us back, we are also ready to set ourselves free. We are ready to pursue more because we know we're capable of having more.

No matter how hard it seems, just know that when your feelings seem as though they are crescendoing and everything is worse than ever, you're probably being set up for a releasing, an awakening, a reconciliation, and the start of the next chapter of your life.

IF YOU DON'T KNOW *what* YOU WANT IN LIFE, START WITH *what* YOU'RE *most* AFRAID *of*

There is nothing more important than knowing what you want in life, and there is almost nothing that is more difficult to figure out.

Until you know what your ultimate goal is—the destination for which you want your life to head—it is almost impossible to start building an existence that supports it. You feel lost. The ordinary ins-and-outs of existence feel empty and the discomfort isn't worth it, because there's no clear payoff in sight.

Until you truly know what you want, you are not going to really achieve anything much at all.

Human beings are exceptional in that we are able to tap into near supernatural strength and willpower when we know what we really want. In fact, when we are clear on what matters, it lights a fire within us that burns every obstacle in the way. There are so many stories of superhuman feats where old women carried pianos out of burning buildings, mothers ripped car doors off to save their kids, and even despite everything going against them, the most truly determined overcame their circumstances and charged ahead toward the life they really wanted to live.

Knowing what you want is half the battle.

Yet, we aren't really coached on how to figure out what we want. We often find it hard to just sit down and imagine what we really crave, as though we have to go searching for it in our subconscious, and all we ever really come up with are bits and pieces that sound nice, and could feel good, but don't really ignite us in that way we need to be lit up.

That's where your fear comes in.

If you do not know what you want, start with what you're most afraid of.

You might not know what you desire, but absolutely everyone knows what scares them.

What is the opposite of that fear?

What is the alternative outcome to your worst-case scenario?

What is the *best possible outcome* for the thing that scares you most?

That is what you want.

That is your true desire, masked behind layers of fear and resistance and conditioning. That is your deep wanting; it has been there all along.

If you are afraid of not having enough money, your desire is financial freedom. If you are afraid of losing love, your desire is healthy, stable relationships. If you are afraid of not having done anything important with your life, your desire is finding purpose in your work, and in your days.

Absolutely everyone knows what they really want—they are just too afraid to want it.

Your desires are not something you have to search for, they are not something you have to generate, or even choose. They naturally exist within you, when you pull back all the layers of fear that are keeping you from them.

We often place fear where desire should be as a way of protecting that desire. We care so deeply, and want it so badly, it becomes too risky for us to acknowledge and lean into it. If we are afraid of it, we are shielding ourselves in a sense, because we aren't even allowing ourselves the chance to fail.

What we do not realize is that this subconscious defense mechanism truly gets us nowhere. It does not keep us safe. In fact, it is the most dangerous coping mechanism, because it leaves us at risk of never truly doing what we came here to do, never really living out our dreams. It robs us of the chance to even pursue those deep desires, because we are in denial about what they really are.

When we know what we want, the path becomes clear, and mountains turn into molehills. Desire is the driving force of our lives, and if you think you can't find it, turn to the shadows of your mind. They are, very often, just trying to dim the light.

SOMETIMES PURPOSE CAN BE *so* SUBTLE, YOU *don't* REALIZE YOU'RE *already* LIVING IT

If you're longing for a sense of purpose, a semblance of meaning, some sort of sign or affirmation that you are, indeed, on the right path, it would probably help to begin with understanding what purpose really is.

Purpose isn't always loud. It also isn't always just one thing. It's not exclusively a job or position, vocation or calling. It's not always your art, it's not always a business, though it can very often be those things. The truth is that your purpose is far more dynamic and deeply embedded within the truth of who you are than you might recognize at first.

Your purpose is something you are already living.

Your purpose is a role you play, firstly, to yourself. It's the relationships you have. It's the way you care for others and they care for you. It's how you exchange love, it's how you bond with some people, and break with others. It's not what you do, but the way you do it. Day in, and day out.

We have all met those human beings that are simply just beacons of kindness, who radiate love through everything they do. We come across them in the most unsuspecting of ways, and yet they very often make such an impression on us, we can remember them to this day.

These are the teachers who gave us guidance, the peers who saw us and stood by us even when we feared they wouldn't. The parent who acted defiantly and taught us the meaning of bravery or loyalty or love. The neighbor who showed us what community means, the random person we passed as we were moving through our errands for the day that gave us a smile or spoke goodness over us, who saw within us more potential than we could have ever initially seen in ourselves.

Our purpose is not just something we do, it's really something we become.

Every time you interact with someone, you are creating a cascading, ripple effect through humanity. You cannot imagine how deeply this web of connectivity is woven, how much a single act of kindness can affect the world at large, how powerfully one soul showing another true love can impact the way that person interacts with every other person they come across—forever.

Imagine the people within your own life who have impacted you the most. Certainly you can see that they weren't always the ones who were doing the work in the most visible ways, but often, the ones who were teaching and showing you unconditional presence. Their purpose was, in part, to be that for you. It was also a thousand other things as well: the kids they taught or patients they nursed, the customers they helped or the partner they loved.

They were able to fulfill those roles because they brought their own unique love to the tasks they were asked to complete within their lifetimes.

In this way, *our first purpose is to ourselves.*

I know that sounds so counterintuitive, as though purpose is exclusively selfless. The reality is that to be overflowing with love, we must first fill ourselves up with it. We must first come to a place of knowing before we can share wisdom. We must first know connection before we can connect. Everyone you admire, who has guided you and loved you into who you are today, did just that.

If your purpose is your job, that is extraordinary.

It is still not your only reason for being.

Your first and most crucial task is your commitment to your own becoming. It is from this garden that all else is harvested.

Your first purpose is just to be here.

To be weird and ordinary and exceptional.

To think and feel and know and wonder.

To build yourself into a person you are proud to be, even if nobody else is clapping for you.

It is only through this that we ultimately share our purpose with every person we know and everyone we someway will. We heal with a simple smile, a message of appreciation, a warm-hearted act of love. We heal as we teach our children and listen to our ancestors. We heal as we learn to take care of ourselves as well as we would any of them.

We heal not as we change what we do upon this world, but how we do it.

We become purposeful as we realize that since the very moment we were born, we were overflowing with potential to extend that love in every direction we can reach.

THIS IS HOW YOU START TO LET GO, *even if* YOU *don't* FEEL LIKE YOU'RE READY YET

You cannot force yourself to let go, no matter how much you know you want to.

You cannot force something out of your brain space, no matter how much you don't want it to be there.

You cannot just simply loosen your grip and relax a little and will yourself to stop thinking entirely about something around which your entire world used to orbit.

This is not how it goes.

You are not going to let go the moment someone tells you to "move on," the day you realize you have to admit certain defeat, the heart-dropping second it occurs to you that hope is, indeed, futile.

You do not let go by willing yourself not to care anymore. This is something that people who have never been painfully hung up on something. This is something that people who have never been deeply attached to something for a sense of safety and security and love and their future believe.

There is nothing wrong with you because you almost feel a sense of anger when people tell you to just "let go" nonchalantly, as though they couldn't fathom the storms in your head and heart.

How can you become so passive about something you have spent so much of your time, and your life, actively working to maintain and restore?

You can't.

You don't.

You start to let go the day you take one step toward building a new life, and then let yourself lay and stare at the ceiling and cry for as many hours as you need.

You start to let go the day you realize that you cannot continue to orbit a black hole in your life, and going on as you were before will simply not be an option.

You start to let go the moment you realize that this is the impetus, this is the catalyst, this is that moment movies are made about and books are written around and songs are inspired by.

This is the moment you realize that you will never find peace standing in the ruins of what you used to be.

You can only move on if you start building something new.

You let go when you build a new life so immersive and engaging and exciting, you slowly, over time, forget about the past.

When we try to force ourselves to "let go" of something, we grip onto it tighter, and harder, and more passionately than ever before. It's like when someone tells you to not think of a white elephant; that's the only mental image you'll be able to focus on.

Our hearts work the same way as our minds in this regard. As long as we are telling ourselves that we must let go, the more deeply we feel attached.

So don't tell yourself to let go.

Instead, tell yourself that you can be upset for as long as you need. That you can fall to pieces and be a mess and let your life collapse and crumble. Tell yourself that you can let your foundation fall through.

What you will realize is that you are still standing.

What you build in the wake and the aftermath of loss will be so profound, so stunning, you will realize that maybe, the loss was part of the plan. Maybe it awakened a part of you that would have remained dormant had you not been pushed the way you were.

If you are certain that you cannot let go of what is hurting you, then don't.

But take one step today, and then another tomorrow, to rebuild a new life for yourself.

Piece by piece, day by day.

Because sooner or later, you're going to go an hour and realize you didn't think about them, or it. Then a day, then a week…and then years and swaths of your life drift by and everything you thought would break you becomes a distant memory, something you look back at and smile.

Everything you lose becomes something you are profoundly grateful for. With time, you see that it was not the path. It was what was standing in your way.

THERE *are* 3 TYPES *of* LOSSES *in* OUR LIVES, *and* *each* TEACHES US SOMETHING DIFFERENT

For as many things as we grow into and gain in life, in equal proportion, we lose, outgrow, and gravitate away from others.

But we don't respond to every loss in the same way. There's a reason why we are so absolutely devastated in the face of some breakups, but neutral if not grateful for others. There's a deep psychological current running beneath the surface of these events in our lives, one that we often aren't conscious of.

There are ultimately three different types of loss that we experience in our lives, and each is meant to teach us something about ourselves.

Heartbreak

Heartbreak is when someone we love doesn't meet our expectations. It's when feelings are not reciprocated, or when someone we care about can no longer be in our lives. Heartbreak makes us feel vulnerable. The "ache" isn't actually that someone has hurt us, rather that we constrict our hearts and want to close off to connection in order to keep ourselves safe.

Heartbreak is painful, but it doesn't make us suffer. Heartbreak is when we get ghosted, when we have a casual boyfriend or girlfriend who moves on. It's when we lose a family member but feel grateful that they are at peace. Though it stings, heartbreak is not an inherently unhealthy thing. It is a natural response to loss. Heartbreak actually teaches us what it means to love, and makes us appreciate what it means to have someone in our lives, because we are now aware of how easy it is to lose them.

Attachment

Unlike heartbreak, the loss of an attachment is when someone we relied on for some fundamental stability or sense of self leaves. It is easy to confuse this for love, but the difference is that when we lose an attachment, we are devastated to the point of feeling unable to function, which usually serves as the catalyst for some kind of radical or sudden self-growth, development, or life change.

When we lose someone we are attached to, we go through a radical process of disintegration, and often experience a drastic shift in our idea of who we are, what we believe, and where we stand in the world. The pain of losing an attachment is actually confronting the fear that we were dealing with before we got attached to the person who is no longer there. That fear usually has to do with feeling unstable, uncertain, or unclear about our future.

Attachment ultimately teaches us who we really are, because in the process of trying to keep the relationship intact, we sacrifice a lot of our own values and sense of self. The extreme pain of a loss of attachment is not the actual loss of the person as it is the loss of what we thought our future would be.

Detachment

Lastly, detachment is what happens when we willingly let go of someone because we recognize that they aren't good for us, even if it means that we hurt ourselves a bit in the process. Detachment comes from real self-awareness and personal evolution. It's when we no longer cling onto what's not serving us just because we are scared.

Detachment can often create heartbreak or the feelings that come with a loss of attachment, but the difference is that this is a separation we initiate because we have enough clarity to realize that the relationship isn't actually good for us. On the other hand, heartbreak and attachment are often the result of being left or abandoned, even if we already know that the relationship isn't working out. Detachment is a sign of maturity, the prioritization of our future selves and our long-term well being.

Detachment teaches us how to love ourselves first. It teaches us how to be resilient. It is a sign that our goal in life is no longer just to remain comfortable. It is the greatest display of self-love. Detaching from a relationship when we know it isn't right is a sign that we no longer rely on others for our sense of stability and self, and it is often the first sign that we are more mentally strong and emotionally free than ever before.

HOW TO WRITE *a* PERSONAL MISSION STATEMENT, *because* YOUR VISION *can become* YOUR REALITY

When it comes to building the life you want to live, most people try to design it backwards.

Most people begin with what habits and routines they want to have each day, as opposed to what habits and routines they would need to start doing to get them where they want to be in five, 10 or 15 years down the line.

This is something called reverse engineering: you have to understand what you want the final product to be before you're going to be able to set all the parts in place to make it happen.

In the same way that companies or schools need to write mission statements, so do you. You need to understand what you want the big, overarching points of your life to be. Otherwise, you'll never really know what you're working toward.

Your mission statement is different from your goals. Your goals are specific, time-particular, measurable accomplishments that you want to achieve by a certain point. They are more rigid, and generally work as a sort of ladder: your goals should be incremental, and one should bring you to the next, and then to the next.

Your mission, however, should be what's at the top of that ladder. Your mission is not necessarily super particular, rather, it can be more fluid, more general, and more descriptive of how you want to feel, not necessarily exactly what you want to do.

Here's an example:

> *I am completely at peace each day. I work two or three days a week consulting in a field that I am passionate about. I have more money than I need, I invest and save wisely, and I keep my living expenses low. I have healthy, loving relationships with my friends and family, I take care of my body and mind each day, and I am confident that I am leaving a positive impact on the world around me, in everything from my daily interactions to the work that I am most proud of.*

Write that down on a piece of paper, post it beside your computer, fold it up and put it in your wallet, and keep it with you at all times.

Your personal mission can help you in the following ways:

01 | You can make better, more aligned decisions.

Let's say you're trying to decide between taking a promotion, or starting your own business. Or you're trying to decide whether you should buy a house where you are, or move across the country. Or on an even smaller scale, you're trying to figure out how to cope with your frustrating relative. When you know what your long-term mission is, you can make these decisions from that perspective. This will help you keep your life on track long-term.

02 | You are writing a blueprint for your brain to adopt.

When you can clearly visualize what your end-goal is, you are giving your brain a sort of blueprint or map of what you want and need it to do.

Remember that so much of your life is habitual: so many of the things you do repeatedly, the things you crave, the things you feel comfortable with are things you've conditioned yourself to prefer, or feel safe doing. You can rewrite these impulses by engaging in new habits and behaviors over time, even though they might feel uncomfortable in the beginning.

03 | You create your own certainty.

More than anything, your personal mission gives you a sense of certainty and stability in a largely chaotic and unpredictable world. It reminds you of what you want to do, who you want to be, and where your priorities need to rest, when it often seems like everyone is trying to pull your attention in every direction.

These are the questions you want to ask yourself to build your own mission:

— *What is it that you want to feel each day?*

— *What do you want to be most proud of by your life's end?*

— *What work do you want to do each day?*

— *How do you want to be remembered?*

— *How do you want to impact others?*

— *How comfortably do you need to live in order to feel whole?*

— Where do you want to spend your days?

— What do you want your relationships to be like?

— What do you want your bank account to look like?

— What do you want your closet to look like?

— What do you want your home to look like?

And you can just keep riffing from there.

Remember that, first, your mission need not be realistic given where you are at right now because you are going to need to think outside of your current circumstances to change your reality. Second, don't expect everything to change instantly. Your life is going to be a gradual, constant unfolding. Third, remember that your mission can change as you do. You are allowed to grow, you are allowed to choose again, you are not beholden to anything you once thought you wanted.

Be free enough to decide who you are and what you really want.

YOU'RE *not* GOING *to* REALIZE YOU'RE BLOSSOMING, BUT *it's* GOING *to* HAPPEN *anyway*

You probably won't recognize the moment you start to change yourself. You probably won't know the day you meet someone who alters the course of your life forever. You might not immediately see the gifts of being brave enough to choose your future self over your current fears.

But it's going to happen anyway.

You're going to blossom anyway because that's what you were designed to do. All of that resistance, that fear, that denial? It's growing pains. It's part of the process.

You're going to be happy and hurting and healing, all at the same time. You're going to see places you never thought you'd see, and still find yourself gravitating to the old ones you thought you couldn't get away from fast enough. You're going to accomplish feats so big and brave you never even dared to dream of them, and you're going to wrestle the same tiny demons that have followed you your whole life. You're going to meet someone who makes you feel more at peace than ever before, and they're also going to shine a bright light on every part you've tried so hard to hide.

Becoming who we are is not a steady, linear ascent into happiness. We don't grow in only one direction. When our lives go bigger, they go outward. We touch more, we feel more, we know more, we see more, we become more.

When we have more to lose, we get scared. When we have to leave our comfort zones, we crave familiarity. No accomplishment, no relationship, no city, no job excuses us from being human. Nothing is going to exempt us from feeling grief when we are sad, anger when we have been dealt an unfair hand, or resentment when we've done too much, and received too little.

This doesn't mean we aren't getting better. This doesn't mean we've backpedaled, or that we're regressing into our old habits. Sometimes, the ability to feel things we haven't thought of in years is the healing. Sometimes, the willingness to cry at something simple and beautiful is the reckoning. Sometimes, befriending ourselves is the most important step of all.

In nature, nothing transforms without breaking first. Flowers can't bloom until they're deeply, wholly rooted. Seasons can't turn until the cold has come and killed off the remnants of the past. Butterflies don't spread their wings before being cocooned up in isolation for weeks, and stars don't become supernovas before facing their own implosion.

Our greatest growth often comes just after we've looked our deepest fears in the eye.

Our most profound advancements are only made possible by the willingness to try, and to fail. When we have nothing to lose, we have everything to gain.

When our hearts are broken and we don't want to be who we once were, we are free to become who we've always wanted. When our dreams are dashed and the future is uncertain, we are no longer beholden to the plan we made for the person we used to be. When something doesn't work out the way we thought, it's almost always because we aren't as good at it as we thought, we don't love it as much as we thought, it wasn't as good for us as we thought.

Becoming is not glamorous. It is not fun. It requires diverging from the easy path, leaving the safe trajectory, risking everything, trying anything.

You will blossom in the moments you are most convinced you are failing and falling behind. When you are jolted awake by your own life, you're on the brink of a personal revolution. It won't be easy, and it won't be beautiful, but you'll get to the other side and realize that all along, there was a reason, there was a rhythm, there was a plan, there was a destination.

You were becoming the person you were always meant to be, even if you didn't realize it at the time. You were growing through the very things you thought were sent to push you off-track. They were, in fact, the ones bringing you back on.

7 THOUGHT PATTERNS *that* ARE KEEPING YOU STUCK *in a* LIFE YOU *don't* WANT

Your thoughts create your perception, which creates your reality.

Your thought *patterns* determine what you think you're capable of, and therefore, what you choose to pursue.

Every time you grow as a person, or your life improves, it happens because you've adjusted or amended a thought pattern. While some of these patterns may be blatantly obvious to you, others are less so. Here are some of the most insidious ideas hindering your potential, often without you ever realizing.

1. "Only so much good can come from my life before it's balanced out by the bad."

When we're young, we lack control over almost every single thing in our lives. We rationalize our near-constant discomfort by believing that life is, in essence, hard.

As we grow up, dramatic and negative events in the world around us affirm this view. We see all the devastating hardships people have to endure and think, *Yes, of course, life is hard!* We're more likely to define the last five years by the one or two "bad" things that happened to us than the literal *thousands* of good things.

This is negativity bias, and it ends up stunting our growth long-term by carrying over into our daily life choices.

We stay at jobs we hate because life is hard. We stay in relationships we are drowning in because life is hard. We think going about our days numb and aggrieved is normal, because again, life is hard.

When our lives begin to tip toward the good, we don't trust it. We assume, after years of prior conditioning, that we're only experiencing a few fleeting positive moments until, inevitably, the rug will be pulled out from under us again.

This isn't so.

When our lives improve—they improve. Good things add up, and we stabilize. The more stable we are, the less likely we are to incur a "negative" experience that's within our control, and the more likely we are to handle one that's out of our control.

2. "I can only earn a life I love by doing things I hate."

The sister belief to, "life is hard and I am simply waiting for my next struggle" is the idea that to have a life we love, we must do things we hate.

If we're never exposed to someone who lives independently, earns money in an unconventional way, or lives in complete peace and true fulfillment, we think those things are impossible. We return to our mindset of checks and balances: *Alright, well, if I want more time and freedom, I need to endure the stress and suffering of work I don't like.*

This is yet another mindset eroding your quality of life.

You cannot hate your way into a life you love. In fact, it's exactly the opposite.

3. "I am responsible for every problem in my proximity."

This is a particularly poignant issue if you're someone with suppressed anxiety. When you have anxiety, you are constantly scanning your environment for potential threats and hazards. When you find one, it becomes your obsession. You fixate on it until you've come up with some kind of emergency plan or otherwise taken control of the situation altogether.

Of course, this works until it doesn't.

It works until you come across a problem that might affect you but is not within your control. Then, you're sent into crisis.

Just because you can empathize with someone's pain does not mean their burden is yours to carry.

Just because you see someone struggling doesn't mean you have to martyr yourself to fix it.

Just because not everyone around you is thriving does not mean you have to hold yourself back.

In fact, the opposite is true.

If you're stunted by the potential negative outcomes of those around you, you will only ever hold yourself back more.

Instead, you must discern the difference between problems you're responsible for and problems you aren't. The difference depends on what's within your sphere of influence. If something isn't—or is, but marginally so—decide on a back-up plan ("this is what I will do in that instance") and move on.

Otherwise, you'll spend your entire life struggling with problems you can't solve, because they aren't really yours.

4. "I cannot ask for an abundant life in a world filled with so much suffering."

So many of us are trapped in the following mindset: *In a world with so much pain and suffering, who am I to ask for a happy and full life?*

The answer is: *Who are you not to?*

By denying yourself fulfillment, are you helping anyone? Are you moving humanity forward? Are you solving the problems that perplex you?

Of course not.

What the world needs is more people with good hearts holding a torch down the paths least taken. We need to prove to each other that happiness is possible, abundance is at our fingertips, and we are allowed to savor every magic moment of our lives.

We do not need more people holding themselves down because of the world's aching. We need more people proving it's possible to dance in spite of it.

5. "Relationships are hard, and they are designed to be that way."

Relationships are not supposed to be hard. They are meant to be challenging, but not excruciatingly painful.

The people in our lives change us, shape us, and create us. If "hell is other people," then heaven probably is, too. Hard patches are inevitable, but relationships are supposed to be a positive force in your life—and if they aren't, it probably means something's awry.

You probably don't think this is possible because you haven't yet been in a relationship that is more flow than friction; you haven't yet met the best friends with whom there's more connection than drama. These are possible, these relationships *exist,* and I know many, many people who have both.

If you don't yet, don't worry. You will.

But you won't if you walk around thinking everyone sucks and people are awful and everyone is going to drive you mad and abandon you eventually. Adjust your perception of relationships, and your relationships will change.

6. "I must be successful to be happy; I must be beautiful to be loved."

I know it seems as though success and happiness are so deeply intertwined that you could not possibly pursue one without creating the other. But our ideas surrounding what it means to be successful in the first place are highly inflated and ultimately pointless.

To be successful is to live on your own terms, to find satisfaction in each day. That's all. Anything else you acquire on top of that is just gravy. It's not the point of your life, it's not a prerequisite for joy.

You do not need to be successful. Similarly, you do not need to be beautiful to be loved.

This is a really harsh way to put it, but objectively un-beautiful people live whole and happy lives and have supportive partners who are passionate about them. Why? Because love is, truly, in the eye of the beholder. Love is so much deeper than surface beauty. And life is so much deeper than success.

Success and beauty, while they fuel the world's most active and aggressive pursuits, are also capitalistic schemes by some measure. They depend on you feeling not quite good enough, so you'll keep investing in improvement—not authentic improvement, but surface-level improvement.

It's a radical act of power to determine that you do not need to be successful, and you do not need to be beautiful. Ironically, accepting this is, in itself, success and beauty in its truest form.

7. "I am the sum of other people's opinions about me."

You probably didn't form your view of yourself independently. In fact, the way you see yourself is probably just the accumulation of the way you think other people perceive you.

Sometimes, you pick up on this through what is said to you or how you're treated. Other times, it's a matter of projection—a metaperception (how you imagine other people view you).

Either way, you are a whole and complete individual that exists outside of other people's perceptions. If you live believing that you're merely the sum of the way you are seen by others, you are going to have a very empty life.

Be alone for a while—intentionally.

Discover who you are when nobody else is around.

Discover what you like when nobody else is there to tell you what to like.

Discover what you want when nobody else is there to tell you what you want.

Discover how you live when nobody else is there to tell you how you live.

When you know who you fundamentally are, on your own terms, you end up shifting the way that the world sees you. Instead of acting in accordance with other people's expectations, you start living up to your own.

YOU *can't* LOSE RELATIONSHIPS, YOU *can only* OUTGROW *them*

If you feel haunted by the loss of a relationship, you are not upset because someone is no longer in your life. You are mourning one idea you had about what your future would look like, and what it means about you that one person you saw in it is no longer there.

The idea that you can "lose" a relationship comes from the idea that you can also "win" a relationship when you're good enough and smart enough and pretty enough and more enough than everyone else who could possibly be a potential partner to the person who chose you.

…And that is not how life works.

You do not lose relationships, you outgrow them. There's no code that says every person you come across is destined to stay in your life forever and ever. In fact, very, very few people will stay with you throughout the duration of your time here.

This is not because you are too flawed to love. This is not because every relationship you have is destined to ultimately break down.

This is because, over the course of your life, you will grow. You will change.

You will be different. Relationships will come into your life and they will run their course and they will change you in some important way and then they will pass.

Relationships are not safeguards against loneliness. You can't whittle yourself down to being as nice and accepting and likable as possible in order to ensure that as many people as possible won't leave you. Relationships come and go; that is what they are designed to do.

Sometimes they leave quickly. Sometimes they leave with a sting. Sometimes they fade, and sometimes you're blindsided by their exit. Sometimes you don't even realize what's happening until it's too late. Sometimes you see the warning signs and dodge a bullet. Sometimes you try to hold on and realize there's nothing left to salvage. Sometimes you choose. Sometimes you don't.

And yet, no matter what, if a relationship leaves your life, there is a reason it has left. There is some part of it you have outgrown, or are no longer benefiting from.

Sometimes you are at fault. Sometimes you are not. Reviewing what happened and taking responsibility for the former is an important part of the healing and growing process.

…But being in pain over every relationship that you no longer have in your life is a waste of your time, and comes from the false belief that if you were good enough, absolutely everybody would stay.

And they wouldn't.

Relationships end when they are meant to end. They are over when they need to be over.

You come into this world alone, and you leave this world alone. Those you meet along the way, however temporarily they remain, are only here to guide you to be more at peace with yourself.

Whatever feelings someone's absence in your life triggers within you is not their problem to resolve. It is yours. It is a hole that you are trying to fill with another person who does not want to play that role in your life, which means that you have no business placing them there, demanding they stay, and blaming them if they don't.

Sometimes, the way that people leave is the lesson itself.

Sometimes, their absence is the experience you need to have in order to reclaim the power in your life.

Sometimes, realizing how you are being selfish and unaware is the greatest gift that someone else can give you, and it will only come when you get the rude awakening you need.

What is no longer a part of your life is no longer a need in your life...even if you can't quite see over the horizon yet.

You are not meant for the people who leave you, you are not always at fault for the people who have left, and you are not broken for those who have faded into the distance. Embracing the ebb and flow of life, and the impermanence of it all, is the way you will learn to love people when you have them and be grateful for them when you don't.

READ THIS *while* YOU'RE WAITING *for the* STORM IN YOUR LIFE *to pass,* BECAUSE *this* COULD BE *the* MOMENT *that* CHANGES EVERYTHING *for* YOU

While you're waiting for this storm to pass, whatever it is, I want you to imagine every other storm you've weathered.

I want you to vividly recall every time in your life you were so absolutely certain that you were entirely screwed, so panicked about how you'd make it through the coming months, so lost that you couldn't fathom what you'd be doing in a year's time.

I want you to imagine everything else you've been through up until this point, every other situation you thought was the end of your entire Universe as you knew it, and recall that there was not one thing you've been through that was worse than the fear that you had about it.

Nothing.

Everything you swore you'd never get over, you did. Everything you were terrified you've never get through, you did. Everything you were certain was going to end your life as you knew it, passed in time.

When you're in a tough or challenging or scary time in your life, you're given an opportunity, and that is to recognize that the storm is on the inside, not the outside. There's nothing you have to run and hide from. The biggest danger you face right now is what you could fail to do out of fear.

Because things happen in life. Relationships end, jobs conclude, loved ones are lost. Cities change, people move, the world spins on.

You're not being punished or tested. You don't need to earn your own peace of mind, or repent for that which you never did.

This could be the moment that changes everything for you because it's only when you're in a storm that you realize you have the power to get out of it.

Not everyone is ready to hear this. Not everyone wants to.

Eventually, you have to realize that the biggest challenge in your life was the state of your own mind. Whether or not it allowed you to enjoy what was in front of you, whether or not it joyfully prepared for the future while savoring today, or whether or not it seized you up and made you feel paralyzed in the face of the unknown.

Change happens to every last one of us. It is the quality of our response to it that determines the degree to which we suffer over it.

There's a saying that when you get to the other side of a storm, you're different, and that's the point of going through it in the first place. But what few people realize is that the storm ends because you're different.

Life shifts in the direction that you do.

The storm often passes when you're done churning the tides.

WE CRAVE PERFECTION *because* WE WANT *to* FEEL SAFE

The truth about perfection is that we only want it so that others might not hurt us for the lack of it.

We don't crave perfection because it's an authentic expression of who we are. We use perfection as a defense not only against other people's potential criticisms, but also against what we know, deep down, is not in alignment in our own lives. It is soothing to make things look just right on the surface when you know that they are wrong just beneath.

Do you really think you need to worry about what someone might think of the small details of your life, or do you need to live in a way that actually makes you feel a little more alive? Do you really want to leave your self-esteem hinging on how you imagine others perceive you, or do you want to find a way to feel proud of yourself at the end of the day? Do you want to arrange your existence so that it would be impossible for anyone to say anything negative about it, or do you want to live with so much joy spilling out from inside you that it renders such opinions meaningless either way?

Letting go of perfection will not make you lose control of yourself. Perfection is a false control to begin with, and letting go of it is you actually re-centering yourself within your own life. It will not hold you back from pursuing what calls you, because what we perceive to be instances of impeccable genius are in actuality moments of the deepest and rawest authenticity—an artist, a person, a partner, a lover, anyone daring to create something or be something that actually makes them feel. It occurs not through a relentless pursuit of what makes us invincible to the world, but finally alive within it.

Perfection and excellence are not the same thing.

One is sought with the intention of how something will appear, and the other is created with the intention of how it will actually be.

There is a reason why we find mountain ranges so vast and so stunning. There is a reason we are moved to tears over a powerful vocal performance, a striking piece of art, why we often stand in reverence of nature or humanity itself.

Beautiful things make us feel at peace, and at ease.

Visually, there is order and sense.

Even when there isn't, there's a magnitude that makes it feel as though it might not have to make perfect sense in order to be extraordinary.

We try to apply the same logic to our lives—that if we could make them appear as though they make sense, they will. However, we approach it the wrong way. The reality is that it is not an image that we can hold within our minds that will put us at ease, it has to be actual, real, raw beauty.

That is often very imperfect.

What we miss is that whatever force created those mountain ranges didn't do it so we'd feel something while we looked at them. The artist themselves had to move past the fear of what we, the audience, might think, and get lost in the song. The point is that none of these things are actually perfect, they have simply been allowed to be.

I hope you find the courage to live an imperfect life.

I hope you begin to see that it was never perfection you were after, perfection was an answer to a question that you were too afraid to ask. Perfection was always the easy way out, the means of convincing yourself that you are enough for your own existence.

I hope you learn to choose what you already know is right.

Not what tells the story of your life most seamlessly, not what you think others would celebrate and cheer for if they discussed it without you in the room, not what you imagine would make for a nice post, the best possible way to sum up your experience, enact revenge on all who ever doubted you, and live happily, albeit one-dimensionally, for the rest of the time you have left.

I hope you begin to see that in place of perfection, you could seek truth.

Truth is high and low, it's messy and it's gorgeous. It's all that's ever mattered. It's living in accordance with your truest values and meeting your deepest needs. It's focusing more on how things look than how they appear.

It is not simply waking up one day and deciding that you will no longer care what anybody else thinks, but determining whose opinions you will value, and whose truly matter. It is not waking up one day and choosing to live mindlessly, with no consideration for how one's actions affect another, but to decide to more consciously rise to the level of your values rather than falling to the level of your reactions. It is not believing that as you make this grand transition into a life that is more fully yours, every person you come across will understand you well, but that whether or not they do is a matter of their own perception, and the quality of your life is going to be a matter of your own.

We are beings designed for connection. We crave it not only to feel safe, but because it is the most essential reality of life—that we, as everything, share a oneness, a sameness that's easy to overlook if you just gaze at the surface. We sever this connection as we try to convince others how worthy we are of their time and attention and love.

That which we seek can only come to us if we connect to ourselves first. It can only exist within our lives insofar as we realize it is our presence that is our greatest value—there is not one additional thing you must do to convince those who are meant to love you that they should stick around. Connection is a self-evident thing, if you're seeking it with those who want to offer it in return.

We get lost because we try to convince those who have no intention of loving us that they should.

In place of a few things that matter, we often seek many that don't. In place of what matters, we crave scale. Without the love of one person we cared for, we want the love of many to make up for it. This is the root from which all perfectionism grows.

You don't look out at the sunrise and wonder if every ray is expressing itself to its fullest potential. You don't criticize the rainstorm for not releasing every drop precisely over the driest ground. You don't sum up other people by how perfectly they do every last thing in their lives. It's their simple presence that makes all of these things beautiful and worthwhile.

Could you learn to see yourself the same way?

HOW *to know if* YOU'RE OVERCORRECTING YOUR LIFE

When you were young, you were taught to override your instincts.

You were born thinking you were okay, and then people started teaching you that you were not okay. Of course, this didn't happen consciously. Over time, you picked up on the rules and expectations around you. You saw what people liked and didn't, who was mocked and who was accepted.

As a kid, you were intrigued by what you saw when you looked in the mirror.

You picked something from the rack at the store and wore it because you loved it.

You felt hungry and you asked to eat.

You had an idea and then acted on it.

You were effortlessly creative, connected, and fundamentally yourself.

Then, when other people started correcting you, telling you how to dress and act and who to be, you began to realize that your essential instincts about yourself were wrong. You disconnected from your natural emotional navigation system. It became clear that you could not be trusted when it came to evaluating the quality of your own life.

As an adult, you probably look in the mirror and don't like what you see.

You pick something from the store based on whether or not it will hide the parts of yourself you hate the most.

You feel a hunger cue and then you question it, and then you question what you want to eat, and then you question whether you should have eaten at all.

You know what you love but don't think you're good enough to do it full time.

You know what you want but wonder what other people would think, and then stop yourself from trying when you assume you'll be humiliated for putting yourself out there.

These are all learned behaviors.

If you are like most people, your standard operating agreement with yourself is that your base instincts are not to be trusted. You believe other people's ideas must be superimposed on top of them.

You think: *If I trusted myself, I would ruin my life.*

You assume that if you really let go—if you really followed your heart and truth—you'd start acting on your emotions and your life would fall apart.

Would it, though? Is that what your most essential, truest, most fulfilled self would do? Probably not. That's the type of behavior we engage in when we've hit our breaking point after so much suppression and disconnection—and we can't help but lash out.

You were taught that your natural instinct is wrong, and that if you started really listening to it, you'd completely let yourself go. This is how societal conditioning works. It relies on you believing that your fundamental self is filled with malice, and that only your self-hate is holding it all together.

In turn, you unlearn how to evaluate what's around you and trust your own assessments and opinions. Then, you end up engaging in one of the sneakiest and most insidious forms of self-sabotage.

When we overcompensate, we try to make up for what we think we lack. When we overcorrect, we try to fix what's broken, even though it isn't.

Overcompensation is a little easier to see. We can kind of sense when someone is so grandiose about their lifestyle that they must, at some level, suffer from a low self-image.

Overcorrecting, however, is sneaky because it can mask itself as humility and self-improvement. In reality, overcorrecting slowly steals your life, keeping you stuck on a cycle of thinking you're not yet good enough.

When we overcorrect, we begin by assuming that every piece of our lives is fundamentally flawed. We think our lives cannot begin until we've fixed everything we can.

Instead of trying to establish a healthy routine, we manipulate our schedule to the very edges of our tolerance and sanity in an effort to be as productive as humanly possible.

Instead of trying to update our appearance, we try to reinvent ourselves as a perfect ideal—and we abstain from life until we have reached that goal.

Instead of trying to develop our relationships, we obsess over who does or doesn't love us, how many friends we have, or the outward appearance of being connected, as opposed to the connections themselves.

Overcorrecting occurs because we do not have a concept of what is "enough" for us.

If someone tells us we need to improve something about our lives, we believe them.

We are so easily sold on this that entire industries are constructed around creating a perceived problem or defect within ourselves, and then selling products to fix the problem they created.

We are easy to manipulate because we no longer have a natural instinct that tells us what would truly feel good in our lives, so we think we have to keep seeking, and keep fixing, until everything is perfect.

The problem isn't that our lives aren't good enough on the outside, the problem is that we were disconnected from our ability to perceive what's enough on the inside. So, we waste money and time and energy and pain on ourselves, hoping that sense of "enough" will somehow come back to us.

Many people really *do* need to change their lives. But if you have a problem, taking action should eventually fix it. That's how you can tell the difference: overcorrecting is a never-ending battle that has no end and never will. Real problem-solving has an endpoint.

This is how we know we are overcorrecting:

— *We are preoccupied with a problem that nobody else seems to think is that bad.*

— *We are so ashamed of this problem we self-isolate and try to hide until it's fixed.*

— *We wait to "begin" our lives until the problem is different.*

— *We are always trying to fix this problem, but it's never really resolved.*

— *No matter how much action we take, we remain close to where we are.*

Overcorrecting can also lead to addictive behaviors, or other forms of self-abuse that either help avoid, distract, or potentially "fix" the issue (think: shopping, or constantly moving to "pursue a new opportunity" but never actually settling).

When we try to overcorrect, we set standards for ourselves that are impossible to achieve because they are fundamentally unhealthy for us to pursue.

This is because, in the past, we behaved in ways we were taught were acceptable—and when that didn't lead to a desired outcome, we learned that *nothing is ever enough.* In turn, we became convinced the only way to exist is to be constantly proving ourselves *to* ourselves.

We started overcorrecting because we were overcorrected.

It is a learned behavior.

When parents or guardians overcorrect, they do so in an effort to avoid connecting with an authentic version of you that makes them uncomfortable (most likely because their own parents reacted similarly to them). Instead, the problem is placed on you.

You are not trying to get better in order to actually *be* better.

You are trying to get better in order to prove to someone else that you're worthy of their attention or love or time.

That is why overcorrecting becomes such a vicious cycle: Your worth is determined by an abstract idea of how you think other people see you, which is a metaperception. You can't know what people really think, so you assume the worst and go from there.

Then you learn hypervigilance. Over time, you recondition yourself to focus so intensely on the negative, you stop seeing anything else.

You adopt the behavior that hurt you so it can no longer be used against you.

You think you're getting ahead of the curve here. If you can identify, list, and try to attack every possible fault someone could find with you, then they cannot disappoint you, reject you, or hurt you. You're pulling an *8 Mile,* your flaws are on the table.

Except this is not how it works, not even a little bit.

You were taught that your imperfections were the reason you couldn't receive connection. In adulthood, you interpreted this as your imperfections being the reason you can't start your life.

You either don't know how to connect, or don't trust connection.

Your life goes on pause, and you scramble to fix a problem that was never a problem in the first place, which means that you're never going to get the result you truly want. You will only ever be frustrated, and waiting.

The root of overcorrecting is not feeling good enough. You don't need to try to force yourself to stop the over-correcting behavior—you just need to teach yourself that you are enough.

This sounds hard, but it's actually simple. Here's how to do it.

1. Reconnect with your honest opinions.

If it's too hard to figure out how you really feel about yourself, start small.

Try new foods and see whether or not you like them. Listen to a new Spotify playlist and decide whether or not you like it. Watch a movie and assess it honestly. Don't think about whether or not someone else approves of it, just focus on how you feel in your body, heart, and mind.

When you start to reconnect with your honest opinions in small ways, you will repair your instincts.

2. Pay attention to your most basic instincts.

Notice when you are hungry, thirsty, or tired.

That's it.

Just make a note of when you're either one of those three things and, when possible, give yourself water, food, and rest.

These survival instincts, unfortunately, get turned off in the overcorrecting process. How many people do you know who are dehydrated, hungry, and exhausted most of the time? Probably a lot.

Start honoring the instincts you know you can sense, and then respond to them accordingly.

3. Grant other people your approval.

This probably seems totally backward, but to feel as though you are enough, you must begin validating other people first.

When you judge other people (which everyone does) you essentially set up a rule for yourself. If you see a successful person, grow envious of them, and then say to yourself, *well, they aren't that great,* you've set the standard that you must now achieve more than them to be good enough.

Over time, this bar goes so high that you cannot possibly reach it.

What you're really trying to do is be better than those people, because you still think worthiness and connection is a competition, a game you can beat.

Instead, if you start supporting, appreciating, and validating people for who they are, how they look, and what they are doing, that grace will naturally extend back to your own life.

4. Stop taking everything personally.

This is what happened when you started overcorrecting in the first place.

People around you projected issues they had with themselves onto you, and then you adopted them as your own.

Someone said: "I'd never wear that," and you took it as: "I shouldn't, either."

You personalized a situation that was not yours to personalize. You did this so often that you ended up governing your life by a set of rules and expectations that aren't yours and never were.

Remember that when other people judge, it's a projection of an issue they have with themselves, in the same way that your worst judgments of other people are projections of issues you have with yourself.

In this way, you can start seeing the origins of your problems less as personal attacks against you and more as, just, you being collateral for someone else's wounding.

You can't stop overcorrecting your life because you can't fix something that isn't broken.

When something in your life really does need to change, you will know.

You will know if you have a real problem, and you will probably be able to sense if you're overcorrecting. You'll sense it because deep down, the little voice you shut out so many years ago is still there, still telling you this truth.

Also: You won't find the energy to fight a battle you don't think is worth fighting in the first place. Instead, you will remain in a state of stress and fear that other people will not agree with you on what's acceptable.

And you're right, some people won't.

But many people will.

When we accept ourselves exactly as we are, something pretty magical happens: We transform into everything we possibly could be.

We cannot hate ourselves into lives we will love.

Releasing the judgment and deciding what's enough for us is the first and most important step to reclaiming our lives as our own.

And if you do want to fix something? Do it from a place of self-respect, not a place of wondering whether or not you will be able to convince the people around you that you are good enough for your own life.

YOU ALREADY KNOW *what* YOUR NEXT STEP IS, YOU JUST *have to* FIND *the* COURAGE *to* TAKE IT

Maybe you don't need to find more answers.

Maybe you don't need to do more soul-searching.

Maybe you don't need more clarity.

Maybe what you really need is the courage to continue, even though the path is no longer new and exciting. Maybe what you need is the resolve to keep stepping forward, even though the process has lost its glimmer, and it has instead been replaced with monotony and routine.

Consciously designing our lives can become a form of escapism. It lifts us right above our lived experience to a place where we believe we haven't quite landed yet, so we haven't really begun. We start to get the idea that we can put ourselves on pause, that we can save up all of the goodness we seek for a later date, when we are better, when things are clearer, when we're better aligned.

This break from our preexisting timeline is absolutely essential, and most people never find the courage to even do it once. Instead, they press on with a life that was chosen for them by their environment, by their peers, by their social expectations, and more than anything, by trying to avoid discomfort and fear.

It is courageous to begin, but most people get stuck again when it's time to simply continue.

Instead of remaining on the journey that's furthering us into alignment with the truth of who we are, the process of discovering more truth can become addicting. We're always one step away from starting, always envisioning some new aspect of a new business, a new opportunity, a new idea, a new plan. We're always wondering when we could take our next trip to a foreign shore to learn something new about ourselves, to bring it back and plant it in the soil of our current lives, and then to see what grows.

Your life is not on pause until you figure everything out.

You don't need to uncover layers upon layers of directives from deep within.

What you find when you escape yourself is the same stuff you're running from in the first place—the only person you're going to wake up and see looking back at you in the mirror is you, no matter where in the world it happens.

The reality is that you probably already know what the next right step in your life is, you just have to find the courage to take it.

I don't mean the courage to leap, endeavor, or try something entirely new.

I mean the courage to wake up every day and stick to the plan.

I mean the courage to face your demons moment-to-moment.

I mean the courage to do what's less gratifying in the moment because it's what's right for you long-term.

I mean the courage to keep going, even in spite of your failures, even though you've messed up, even despite the fact that you very well might do so again.

I.mean the courage to embrace your humanness.

I mean the courage to accept that not every day is a good day, even when you're living the life of your dreams.

I am not talking about the courage to leap and build your wings on the way down, but the courage to keep stepping forward, even though it's hard, even though you're tired, even though it feels as though the world is crashing down on top of you, even though it's unfair, and even though you'd very much rather numb it all out and avoid everything altogether.

The next right step in your life is not always the one that scares you the most.

Sometimes, it's the one that bores you the most.

Sometimes, it's the least exciting option.

Sometimes, it's the one that you're avoiding, resisting and running away from, because it's the step that requires you to sit in your discomfort, metabolize your uncertainty, and do what you know you will have wished you did a few years down the line.

I'm talking about self-discipline.

I'm talking about vision.

I'm talking about not confusing the forest for the trees.

Because at the end of the day, almost every single one of us knows what the right thing to do is, the journey is developing the courage, bravery, resolve and willingness to do it again, and again.

It is not always about how we can start over, but how we might just show up.

It's not always about reaching the mountaintop, but sometimes just being willing to take a few steps on the path and know that it is enough.

It is not that your life can never be exciting, just that most of us are under the unrealistic delusion that everything must be a peak experience all of the time. This leads us to a process of constantly uprooting, which is the self-sabotaging behavior of planting seeds, sprouting them, and then starting all over again.

What we need is not always the courage to disrupt the status quo, but rather, to stay on the new path we've chosen for long enough that we can build the new patterns we seek, create the new normal we desire, and finally see the results that we know are possible if only we can navigate through the moments when we aren't inspired.

Nobody feels inspired all of the time.

It's not about waiting until you feel ready.

It's about doing it anyway, and knowing readiness will come.

I HOPE YOU LEARN *how to* *gently* START OVER

Your life will be a series of inhales and exhales, and I don't mean how your body consumes oxygen and expresses carbon.

I mean that becoming yourself is a series of building and undoing, trying and failing, showing up, and sometimes, turning away.

Because when we do not know how to gently start over, then we do not know how to live.

Nobody was meant for one path.

It's only how we respond to the moment, how we adapt, how we inch closer to our truest selves, that we ever start to feel as though we know why we are here.

I hope that you learn how to gently start over.

I hope that you learn how to look at yourself and know that you aren't quite the person you want to be, without condemning the person you currently are. I hope you learn how to see your evolution not as a linear ascent into perfection, but an unpacking of why you might want to perfect yourself in the first place. What feels so broken? And who taught you it was that way?

I hope that you learn success is less about vision than it is consistency, because ideas are easy, and everyone has them. It is what you act on consistently that you truly see the viability of. It is what you do all of the time that you learn to grow around and through. You are not supposed to get it all right the first time, you're just supposed to keep trying until you do.

I hope you learn that loving is much like life—it takes everything and gives everything back. And merging your life with someone else's is the greatest honor you'll ever get, so I hope that you learn how to bend, not break, how to compromise, not take, and how to appreciate, not assume.

I hope you learn that you are also your own project, your own muse, your own love affair.

I hope you learn you belong to yourself.

I hope you learn that you are not meant to grow once and never again, but to fall in love with the process of building, and pulling apart, and rebuilding again.

Life calls us to shed ourselves at different points in time.

There is nothing we can do to avoid this—no dogma, no religion, no belief, no accumulation of belonging that could possibly remove this requirement from us.

We are not here to be just one person, nor a series of ourselves piled up upon one another, fighting for relevance and dominance and space.

We die and are reborn often.

Instead of gripping tightly to that which gives you a place, I hope you learn that growth is really just learning to love what you have while you have it, be where you are while you're there, and not get too flustered at the fact that you're still a work in progress.

There is no point at which you are supposed to be completed.

The only finish point is death.

Your life is about gently starting over, every day, every hour, in ways both subtle and disruptive, beautiful and melancholy, startling and expected.

I hope you learn how to gently dust yourself off and begin again, because life is too short to stay stagnant, life is too full to only drink a quarter of the glass.

ABOUT *the* AUTHOR

BRIANNA WIEST is the bestselling author of *101 Essays That Will Change The Way You Think* and *The Mountain Is You*. Her work on mindfulness, spirituality and self-improvement has appeared in publications such as *Forbes, The Huffington Post, USA Today* and *Thought Catalog,* where she is currently a partner. Brianna is also the author of two poetry collections, *Salt Water: Poems On Healing & Wholeness,* and *Ceremony: Poetry & Prose.* Her life's work is to help people activate their potential by rewriting their inner narratives with more alignment, truth and purpose.

briannawiest.com
twitter.com/briannawiest
instagram.com/briannawiest

MORE FROM

BRIANNA WIEST

CEREMONY

SALT WATER

THE MOUNTAIN IS YOU

I AM THE HERO OF MY OWN LIFE

101 ESSAYS THAT WILL CHANGE
THE WAY YOU THINK

THOUGHT
CATALOG
Books

BROOKLYN, NY